Critical Praise for
Best Websites for Financial Professionals,
Business Appraisers, and Accountants

"This is a highly practical reference tool for any business appraiser or financial advisor. The authors are two of the best-known business valuation research professionals in the United States."

Shannon Pratt, CFA, FASA, MCBA
Managing Director
Willamette Management Associates

"This book will save the appraiser significant time when looking for pertinent data. A great resource to increase the quality of work product and credibility of the appraiser's conclusions."

Michele G. Miles, Esquire
Executive Director
Institute of Business Appraisers

"An exceptional compilation of resources available to those looking for financial and industrial information on the Internet. Those quite experienced with Internet research as well as those just starting out will find helpful information in this book."

Lisa Doble Johnson
Vice President Research
Mercer Capital

THE BEST WEBSITES FOR FINANCIAL PROFESSIONALS, BUSINESS APPRAISERS, AND ACCOUNTANTS

THE BEST WEBSITES FOR FINANCIAL PROFESSIONALS, BUSINESS APPRAISERS, AND ACCOUNTANTS

EVA M. LANG
JAN DAVIS TUDOR

John Wiley & Sons, Inc.

NEW YORK • CHICHESTER • WEINHEIM • BRISBANE • SINGAPORE • TORONTO

This publication is designed to provide accurate and authoritative information in regard to the subject matter covered. It is sold with the understanding that the publisher is not engaged in rendering legal, accounting, or other professional services. If legal advice or other expert assistance is required, the services of a competent professional person should be sought.

Library of Congress Cataloging-in-Publication Data

Lang, Eva M.
    The best websites for financial professionals, business appraisers, and accountants / Eva M. Lang, Jan D. Tudor.
      p. cm.
   ISBN 0-471-37157-2 (pbk. : alk. paper)
   1. Business—Computer network resources—Directories.   2. Web sites—Directories.   3. Internet—Directories.   I. Tudor, Jan D.
II. Title.

HF54.56 .L36 2001
025.06'65—dc21   00-054562

Printed in the United States of America.

10 9 8 7 6 5 4 3 2 1

About the Authors

Eva M. Lang, CPA, ASA, is a nationally recognized expert on electronic research for business valuation and litigation support services. She is a frequent speaker to national groups on technology issues and is a contributing editor for *The CPA Expert,* published by the American Institute of Certified Public Accountants. She currently serves as Chief Operating Officer of the Financial Consulting Group, the largest alliance of business valuation and consulting firms in the United States.

Jan Davis Tudor is President of JT Research, located in Portland, Oregon. Jan considers herself a freelance research librarian, and while her business caters to business appraisers, she researches a wide variety of subjects. She received her master's in Library and Information Studies from the University of California at Berkeley, and is a member of the Association of Independent Information Professionals and the Special Library Association. Jan has been a speaker on research strategies and Internet, both nationally and internationally, and is a columnist for *EContent* magazine. She loves living in the Pacific Northwest with her husband, dog, and cat.

Acknowledgments

Eva:
A special note of thanks to the executive board of the Financial Consulting Group for their support, to the Messengers Sunday School class of Christ United Methodist Church Memphis, Tennessee, for their prayers, and to Barbara Walters Price, Vice-President of Marketing for Mercer Capital, for her encouragement and advice. I am also deeply indebted to my husband and partner, Scott LeMay, without whom this book would not exist.

Jan:
Many thanks to my dear husband, Greg, and friends Karin, Vivian, Margery, Jennifer, Jacqueline, Lyda, and Joan for being there. A kind "thank you" to Sujin Hong of John Wiley & Sons, Inc. for her remarkable editing skills.

Contents

Foreword

by James L. (Butch) Williams
Director, Dixon Odom PLLC Business Valuation
& Litigation Services
Chairman, AICPA Business Valuations Subcommittee

I have always greatly admired those courageous individuals who are willing to lead with their hearts while others reside in the shadows of anonymity to critique and question, and it came as no surprise to me that Eva Lang and Jan Tudor would be the first to lead our profession with a definitive guide to navigate the vast Internet. The art of technology is successfully transforming modern life. Nowhere are the possibilities more apparent than in the business valuation arena.

Well grounded in library science and research fundamentals, this treatise is not just an essential, technically valuable tool, but rather it avails to the reader a wealth of practical application garnered from many years of performing financial and valuation engagements. These are two highly educated and intelligent professionals, yet because of their varied experience, their feet are firmly planted in the world of engagement reality. The resultant text magically weaves the technical and practical to provide just the right fabric of information to ably serve both the most seasoned veteran and the practitioner just entering the research arena. Jan and Eva are trained experts who are passionate about what they do, and this excellent joint offering serves as their special gift to better the profession.

As valuation professionals, we are keenly aware that almost every opinion we submit will be met, at some point, with intense scrutiny and aggressive opposition. To successfully defend against those affronts, we must perform our services thoroughly and effectively. The information gathering process is a critical component of every valuation, and the volume of available research is staggering. Few of us can afford the luxury of trained professional researchers in our organizations, yet the technical demand to correctly canvas the available data and information requires us all to undertake as exhaustive a search as possible in every engagement. However, thoroughness must also blend with its practicality engagement partner, and practitioners are continually seeking to find the most direct, cost-efficient routes to the proper information for their particular project. This text provides the right solution in achieving this highly desired balance. What you will find in this instructive work is a labor of love, painstakingly compiled and wonderfully communicated. It is rich with educational content and shared wisdom, and it is a useful tool that financial and valuation analysts have sought for quite some time.

To safely navigate the perilous waters of the Internet requires a compass that is reliable and well tested. Many years of research, financial training, and experience have empowered Eva and Jan with wisdom and skills that they now graciously share with us in written form. For those of you fortunate enough to have participated in seminars and speeches given by them, you will recognize a bountiful list of materials that have withstood the test of time in this rapidly changing environment—yes, though the available Internet data has changed dramatically, there are still plenty of foundational sites that every financial and valuation analyst should consider in performing their research duties. This text generously provides a wealth of them for your benefit.

It is an immensely bold effort to attempt to capture the best Internet resources for business appraisers, accountants, and financial professionals. Yet, we are fortunate, indeed, that the two best-qualified professionals to accomplish this daunting task just happen to be the two that are the most passionate and knowledgeable about the subject. Their book is an indispensable manual that will powerfully equip you to meet your research practice challenges.

Preface

The Internet is a rich source of financial and industry information. In fact, there are more finance, investment, and industry-related sites than just about any other kind of site except for, perhaps, those offering other types of "adult entertainment." This book attempts to pull together the most useful of the financial sites in a single volume directed at the financial professional. The sites included in this book are the result of years of collective Internet research, and we are sharing the sites we consider the cream of the crop. By learning and bookmarking these selected sites, you will be off to a great start with your research projects.

This book is aimed primarily at the accountant or financial analyst who is engaged in consulting work, such as business appraisal, financial planning, and management consulting. The consulting area is the most rapidly growing area of accounting practice, and financial professionals in this area can benefit significantly from the increase in information available on the Internet.

Using the Internet is potentially one of the most efficient ways to conduct research for business valuation information. Traditional newspaper and magazine publishers, trade associations, consulting firms, governments, and individuals are placing enormous amounts of valuable information on the Internet. With each passing year the number of printed resources that do not have electronic versions accessible on the Web is shrinking. As a result, the Internet has become particularly valuable for researching companies, industries, and markets.

Since our focus here is on Internet resources, we have not covered in much detail major commercial information providers such as Lexis/Nexis, WestLaw,

Dialog, Profound, OneSource, and Dow Jones Interactive or financial data services such as Bloomberg and Securities Data. Historically, these providers targeted information professionals at large corporations and libraries with very expensive, proprietary, dial-in (not Internet-based) services. These services were typically difficult to learn and rarely used directly by financial professionals.

That scenario is changing, as more and more providers are now targeting end users, changing pricing schemes to appeal to smaller firms, making searching easier, and packaging content in more "user-friendly" ways. Long the "gold standard" for information gathering, these services still contain some of the best information available. In many cases, information found on services such as Lexis/Nexis and Dialog is not available elsewhere on the Web.

We strongly encourage you to consider subscribing to one of these services if you find that your information needs are increasing and can no longer be met by free and low-cost websites. It is important to reiterate that, despite popular belief, everything ever published is not available on the Internet, and that not all information on the Net is free. In addition, because time is valuable, it may make more sense to spend five minutes on a fee-based service and pay for the data rather than spend hours trying to find it for free on the Net.

Efficient and effective Internet research also depends on the skill of the researcher. It takes time to develop a "feel" for the Internet and know where to turn for information. Even though we devote a lot of our time to research, we still find it challenging to keep up with the changes in sources as well as search tools and techniques. Because it is so important to know how to use the tools that will help you find information on the Internet, we start this book with a chapter on search engines. While you may bookmark many (if not all) of the sites in this book, chances are that you will still need to use search engines and directories to find additional material for a specific research project.

If you wonder why just a handful of sites are suggested for a specific subject, it is most likely because the site mentioned is considered a "portal." In order to keep visitors on their sites and, it is hoped, increase profitability and brand recognition, Internet companies are converting their sites into portals, or "one-stop-shopping" sites, for researchers. A clear example of a portal is the familiar Hoover's. Years ago Hoover's provided strictly financial information on publicly traded companies. In order to find news about a particular company, researchers would have to switch over to another site.

Now researchers can find a broad range of company information at Hoover's and not need to leave the site, because over the years the company made alliances with other information companies, such as Powerize and Reuters. We believe that well-designed and content-rich portals are extremely valuable because they save the researcher time and therefore money. A large number of the sites mentioned in this book are portals, and we highly recommend getting to know them.

In addition, as can be expected, there has been some fallout on the Internet. Some excellent sites, such as Deep Canyon, simply lost their funding, and some of those with less valuable content folded. It appears that the strong sites just keep getting stronger—once again, Hoover's comes to mind.

Finally, while every attempt was made to provide up-to-date information, the rapid pace of change on the Internet makes that virtually impossible. Be aware that website addresses may have changed along with the amount and cost of the content on each site.

Eva M. Lang and Jan Davis Tudor
Memphis, Tennessee and Portland, Oregon
October 2000

THE BEST WEBSITES FOR FINANCIAL PROFESSIONALS, BUSINESS APPRAISERS, AND ACCOUNTANTS

CHAPTER 1

Searching the Internet

Eva M. Lang

I have yet to meet an Internet user who did not have a horror story about the difficulty of finding information on the Internet. For financial professionals, the inability to find information quickly and efficiently is not just inconvenient; it costs real dollars in lost billable time.

Why do so many people have problems finding information on the Internet? Part of the problem is the rapid growth of the Internet. According to a study by the NEC Research Institute, 25 new Web pages are added to the Internet every *second*.

Another reason can be found in a recent Outsell survey that found 66 percent of Web researchers have no search training. Interestingly, the same survey found that 96 percent of Internet users consider themselves "skilled" or "very adept" at finding information, leading us to the conclusion that Internet users are delusional.

In both cases, the problem can be managed (if not solved) by choosing the right search tools. In most cases, it is not that the facts are unavailable. It is that the wrong search tools fail to find the desired information or that searchers do not know how to use the tools.

Having the right tool for the job can make many processes go more smoothly. That applies to carpentry, cooking, and Internet searching. A specialty search engine that limits searches to specific topic areas, such as law, business, and medicine, is often the right search tool for financial professionals.

Searching the Internet has been likened to finding a needle in a haystack. Specialty search tools are not perfect, but using them is like searching for a bigger needle in a smaller haystack. (Actually, according to the specialty search engine Cliché Finder at *www.westegg.com/cliche*, the whole needles-and-haystack thing has been done to death, and we have to stop using that phrase.)

What exactly is a specialty search tool and why should you use one? A specialty search engine does not attempt to catalog the entire Internet. It focuses on a niche area. Examples are search engines that only search for news stories or for stock quotes.

There are several reasons to give them a try. Chances are that a focused search on a niche topic will take less time than a search using a general search tool. You will get fewer hits and you can review them more quickly. An example is a search for the term "beta." Searching for "beta" in a general search engine will get you 976,403 hits equally divided between fraternity home pages and pages where computer companies offer beta versions of software. The same search in a financial search engine will yield 150 hits, and all the hits will be about investment risk.

Also, in many cases the quality of the search results is higher because many specialized search engines manually choose their entries. An example is the legal directory FindLaw, which has humans review all the sites it catalogs. That means their reviewers eliminate Joe's Bait, Tackle, and Legal Services from the site before you ever see it.

Specialty search engines often index sites that general search engines do not cover. This is because they may solicit sites from users or knowledgeable reviewers who know whether the sites are relevant. Some specialty search engines even rank the sites they index.

Despite the benefits that specialty search engines offer, they are not always the best choice in every search situation. Sometimes a general search engine, such as Google or Hotbot, will work better. Bigger is better if you are looking for obscure information or even anything that's relatively uncommon.

Because there is surprisingly little overlap among search engines, you can improve your chances of finding what you want by searching with more than one search engine. One way to do this is with a metasearch tool. Metasearch engines are designed to search multiple search engines and directories and return the results in a consolidated format.

Of course, it does not matter how many search engines you try if you do not structure your search well. This is where a little search training can offer a big payoff. Many searchers just type in a keyword without thinking about how they can work with the logic of the search engine to get better results. For example, if you search on a phrase like "intellectual property," most search engines will not know that you want documents in your search results to contain those two words in that order. Most search engines will look for records containing either "intellectual" OR "property," which is why you will wind up with 795,302 hits.

To improve the quality of your search results, you must know what advanced search features each search tool supports and how to use them. For many search engines, just putting the search phrase in quotes is all that is necessary to tell the search engine to find records containing the phrase. But what if your results consistently contain a phrase that you do not want? For example, you are searching on the keyword "compensation" because you are looking for a salary survey to prove how underpaid you are, but all the search results are websites about how to apply for workers compensation insurance. Here is where it would be very helpful to know about Boolean logic and to have a search engine that uses it.

The principles of Boolean logic refer to the logical relationship among search terms. The Boolean operators that express these relationships are AND, OR, NOT, and NEAR. In the compensation example, clearly you are not the least bit interested in "workers compensation," so if we eliminate the records that contain the word "workers," you would have a better chance at finding that salary survey to justify your raise. Assuming the search engine supports Boolean logic, we can type in "compensation NOT workers" and get the desired result.

The other Boolean relationships work in a similar manner. The search term "option AND model" will return records that contain both terms somewhere in the record. The search for "accounting OR auditing" will return records that contain either term and "industry NEAR trend" will find records where the two terms are less than a specified number of words apart.

Other advanced search features that can help improve your searches include field searching and truncation. Field searching simply refers to limiting a search to a particular field in the record. Many search engines support URL (Uniform Resource Locator) field searching, which allows you to search on all or part of a domain name. For example, typing in the term "URL: IBM" would find all the URLs for IBM. Another common field to search is title, so the search term "title:valuation" would return results only where "valuation" appears in the title of the document or Web page. Truncation or wildcard searching refers to searching on variations of a root word. The asterisk is a common wildcard symbol. Typing in the search term "valu*" would return records containing value, valuation, and valuing.

Some search tools do not support full Boolean searching but may support implied Boolean searching. This implied Boolean searching, or "Boolean Lite," substitutes the symbols "+" or "−" for the operators AND and NOT.

While the search terms you select can influence the quality of the search results, the order in which the engine presents its results to you is also critical to the success of your search.

All search engines rank their results according to sets of rules for relevancy. One of the primary determinants of relevancy is the location of your search term in the record searched. Web pages with search words in their titles are assigned higher relevance than pages that have the word in the body of the text. In the past, the frequency of appearance of the search term affected relevancy. But once Web page designers realized this and started repeating keywords hundreds of times in order to get a higher ranking, most search engines stopped using this to rank pages.

Relevancy rules vary among search engines. Some engines rank sites according to the number of other sites linked to them or by how frequently previous searchers visited them. Some search engines rank sites based on payments from advertisers, so an advertiser's site will be ranked first regardless of the quality or the popularity of the site.

Sometimes even picking the best specialty search engine and crafting the perfect search terms are not enough to find the information you need. A search engine cannot find some things:

- The content in sites requiring a log-in for access
- Certain types of file formats, such as Adobe Portable Document Format (PDF), which retains the original page layout, including tables and charts.
- Pages that are not generated until the user completes a form
- Databases
- Intranets; pages not linked from anywhere else
- Sites with domain limitations or antirobot software

Unfortunately, the more valuable the information, the more likely it is to be hidden from search engines. Some searchers refer to this data hidden from search engines as the "invisible Web." The hidden data tends to be information like the Securities and Exchange Commission's EDGAR filings by public companies that are in a database on the SEC site. You cannot use a regular search engine to find the 10-K filing for Federal Express because the 10-K resides in a database and a form must be filled out to request the document on the SEC site. The good news is that there is an interest in these invisible Web resources, and tools are being developed to identify and locate such documents.

All sites are presented in alphabetical order. The sites listed in the "First and Foremost" section of this chapter are those that the authors have found to be reliable, well organized, and rich sources of information. Sites offering all or part of the data for free are considered more desirable than sites offering similar data for a fee. "Best of the Rest" sites may focus on a niche area, be fee only, or have limited navigation and output features.

In this chapter you will see an additional comment below the title of the site indicating whether this is a general or specialty search tool. As discussed earlier in this chapter the specialty tools focus on a niche area while the general search tools can be used to research a variety of nonfinancial sites as well.

FIRST AND FOREMOST

About.com

www.about.com (Exhibit 1.1)

Type: Specialty

Free site

About.com is a directory of 700 specialty websites, each focused on a single topic and grouped into 36 channels (arts and literature, education, hobbies, shopping, sports, etc.).

About.com uses actual humans to do a job often performed by computers. A human guide manages each specialty site. The guides create original content

Exhibit 1.1 About.com

for their websites and maintain Internet directories, e-mail newsletters, bulletin boards, and chat rooms in their topic area. The company's editorial staff monitors each site.

The coverage in any area is dependent on the quality of the guide. As of this writing there is no guide for the accounting site at *http://accounting.about.com*, so that area is not updated. However, the taxes site is current and well maintained at *http://taxes.about.com*.

On the other hand, there are a number of industry sites with excellent guides and great content. For example, the Beverage Industry site at *http://beverage.about.com*, the Waste Management Industry site at *http://wastemanagement.about.com*, and the Construction Industry site at *http://construction.about.com* all have knowledgeable guides with relevant industry experience who have assembled useful collections of information about their respective industries.

Fast Search

www.alltheweb.com   (Exhibit 1.2)

Type: General

Free site

At the time of this writing, Fast Search claimed to be the world's largest search engine, with over 575 million full-text Web documents. While the "world's largest" title has been passed among several general search engines, few have pursued it with the single-mindedness of Fast Search. Fast Search entered into a partnership with Dell in early 1999 with the announced goal of building the world's largest search engine, and it has pursued that goal ever since. At the time that Dell came on board, Fast Search indexed just 80 million Web pages.

Initially, Fast Search just offered one general search engine. Following an investment by Lycos in 2000, Fast Search added three specialty search engines that limit searches to FTP (File Transfer Protocol) files, MP3 music files, or multimedia files using Lycos technology. Fast search has also added a WAP (Wireless Application Protocol) search for users of wireless, hand-held, Internet-enabled devices.

Fast Search's advanced search features include field searching, language, and domain limits. Users can enter three separate search terms or keywords and mark each as "Should Include," "Must Include," or "Must Not Include," but full Boolean searching is not supported. Users can limit searching to any of 31 different languages. A domain filter allows users to limit results to a particular domain.

Exhibit 1.2 Fast: All the Web. All the Time™

FindLaw

www.findlaw.com   (Exhibit 1.3)

Type: Specialty

Free site

FindLaw is a directory of legal resources. The site may look familiar because it is based upon the Yahoo Internet Directory design. The FindLaw site began in 1995 as a list of Internet resources compiled for a workshop of the Northern California Law Librarians. Since then the site has evolved into a guide to legal information that includes more than 25,000 (human-edited!) site listings. Find-Law covers both primary sources (e.g., codes, cases, statutes) and secondary sources (e.g., law journals, commentary). FindLaw also provides online access to a number of specialty guides on topics such as constitutional law and cyberspace law. The separate FindLaw Library at *http://library.findlaw.com* is a full-text searchable database of more than 10,000 documents on 200 different topics published by bar associations, legal publishers, prominent law firms, and the federal government.

Exhibit 1.3 FindLaw
Copyright FindLaw, Inc.

In addition to browsing the listings in the FindLaw directory, users can enter a simple search using the search box at the top of the home page. However, the best way to search FindLaw is by using LawCrawler, which is accessible from either a button on the home page or directly from its unique URL at *http://lawcrawler.findlaw.com.* LawCrawler is a powerful legal Web search tool that reaches beyond FindLaw to search the entire Internet for legal resources. LawCrawler supports Boolean operators and searching can be limited to specific databases.

FindLaw has developed a site for small businesses at *http://smallbiz. findlaw.com,* called the FindLaw Small Business Toolkit. This site provides information on starting, financing, managing, and marketing a small business. Resources include a guide to small business websites, business and legal news, step-by-step checklists, sample business plans, and downloadable forms and legal documents.

FirstGov

www.firstgov.com   (Exhibit 1.4)

Type: Specialty—Federal Government

Free site

A new U.S. government website was launched in September 2000. The ambitious mission of this new site, FirstGov, is to provide one-stop access to all federal government online information and services. The idea is to make it easy to search for government information and services by topic rather than by agency. In the past, it was often necessary to know what agency or governmental unit produced a certain document and to go to that agency's website to find it. Because FirstGov has access to all government Web pages, it is no longer necessary to know which agency holds what information.

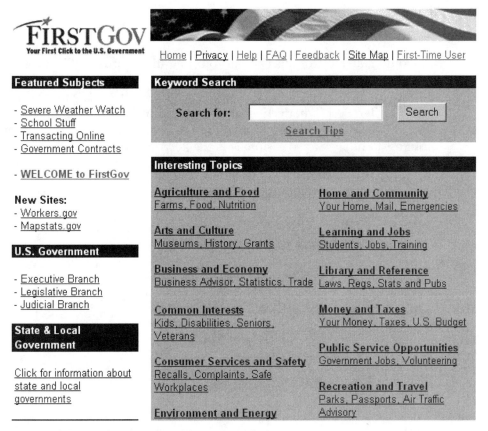

Exhibit 1.4   FirstGov: Your First Click to the U.S. Government

FirstGov's powerful search engine can search 27 million federal agency Web pages.

FirstGov has few advanced search features but does support wildcard searching and field searching by URL. Users can search for an exact phrase by using quotes around the phrase.

FirstGov is a new site and not all the kinks are worked out. While the site has succeeded in organizing a directory of government sites without using the agency structure, it is still not an intuitive arrangement. Users may want to consider also using the Google Uncle Sam site at *www.google.com/unclesam* or the Northern Light USGovsearch site at *http://usgovsearch.northernlight.com/ publibaccess* to supplement a search for government information.

Google

www.google.com   (Exhibit 1.5)

Type: General

Free site

It would take most of this chapter to list all the awards that Google has won. The short list would include "Best Technical Achievement Webby Award," "Best Search Engine on the Internet" by *Yahoo! Internet Life* magazine, one of the "Top Ten Best Cybertech of 1999" by *TIME* magazine, the "Technical Excellence Award" from *PC Magazine,* and "Best Search Engine" by The Net. Of interest to financial professionals is the 2000 study done by the independent research firm FIND/SVP that named Google the number-one search engine for business research.

Why has Google attracted so much attention since its launch in 1998? In a nutshell, it is Google's consistent ability to return the most useful and relevant sites. Like many other general search engines, Google's search engine relies on software that retrieves Web pages based on word placement. The addition of proprietary technology called PageRank greatly increases the relevance of the sites returned. PageRank finds Web pages based on the number and quality of other Web pages that point to it. PageRank treats ranking as a popularity contest so that pages with lots of links pointing at them or a few links from important Web sites are ranked high.

Advanced Search - Language, Display, & Filtering Options

| Google Search | I'm Feeling Lucky |

Google index: 1,060,000,000 web pages

New! Use Google to get stock quotes - just enter a ticker symbol.

Cool Jobs - Try our Web Directory - Advertise with Us
Add Google to your Site - Google Browser Buttons - Everything Else

Exhibit 1.5   Google
Courtesy of Google, Inc.

Ixquick

http://ixquick.com   (Exhibit 1.6)

Type: Metasearch

Free site

Ixquick is one of the best search engines you have never heard of. It is a meta-search engine that searches 14 major search engines including Altavista, Excite, Fast Search, Snap, Hotbot, and Yahoo! Ixquick distinguishes itself in several ways that make it one of the best metasearch engines currently available.

It scores websites based on how the underlying search engines rank the site. Sites that rank in the top 10 in the underlying search engine get a star from Ixquick. Ixquick also eliminates duplicate hits, so you have a clean list of results.

It formulates searches tailored to the requirements of each search engine. Because each search engine treats Boolean operators differently, submitting the same search to all the engines could miss some important sites. Ixquick knows which search engines can handle wildcards and other advanced search features and translates and forwards your searches exclusively to those search engines that can respond to them properly. This allows for more relevant results without requiring the user to learn the intricacies of each search engine.

Exhibit 1.6 Ixquick
Courtesy of Surfboard Holding, B.V.

Ixquick allows users to search the Web and also newsfeeds, MP3 files, and images. It supports searching by fields (title, domain, host, image, URL, link, text, and related) as well as natural language queries and Boolean search terms.

JustQuotes

www.justquotes.com   (Exhibit 1.7)

Type: Specialty—Financial

Free site

Justquotes is the financial data search engine owned by Red Herring, the business technology publishing company. Despite the name, Justquotes is more than that; it is an aggregator of financial information for public companies and mutual funds. Instead of going to one site for a company profile, another for stock quotes, and yet another for research, you can cover all the bases at Justquotes.com.

Enter a company name or stock symbol, and you'll be linked to a page with quotes, financial data, and related websites. Type in "FDX" (Federal Express) and find current and historical stock prices, news stories, analyst's recommendations, and earnings estimates from C-Net, Zacks, Quicken, Morningstar, Market Guide, and other sources. Justquotes presents all this free data on a single page along with links to company financial records and Securities and Exchange Commission filings.

FEDERAL EXPRESS (FDX)
Add to My Portfolio

quote | chart | newsbureau | historicals | **research sheet**

As of...	Last Price	Change	52-Week High	52-Week Low	P/E Ratio	Market Cap.	Shares Outstanding
close on Oct 17	**40.2200000**	-0.8800000 (-2.14%)	47.9300000	30.5600000	16.0	$11.464B	285.038M

Navigation Bar — At Your Fingertips | Charts | Competitors | Discussion Forums | Earnings | Financial Ratios, Measures & Indicators | Financial Statements | Historical Prices | Insider Info | News | Profiles | Quotes | Recommendations | Sec Filings | Splits, Dividends & Buybacks | Stock Returns

at your fingertips - FDX

detailed quote
option quote
livet chart screen

newsbureau
news

hoovers profile
yahoo! profile
zacks profile

discussion forum
competitors
insider trades

stock analysis
analyst recommendations
earnings growth/history
earnings release date
upgrades
downgrades

balance sheet
income statement
cash flow analysis
financial ratios
stock report

sec filings
annual report

1 month chart - FDX

hi 45.04

lo 38.10

STOCKMASTER

charts - FDX

Exhibit 1.7 Justquotes.com
Courtesy of Stockmaster.com

Moreover

http://w.moreover.com

Type: Specialty News

Free site

Moreover is an online news aggregation service. Founded by a *Financial Times* reporter and now backed by Reuters, Moreover searches more than 1,500 editorial sources to provide Web feeds of headline links. Some of these are standard or specialty news sites, such as CNN or CBS Marketwatch. Others are not strictly news sites but have current information about a particular subject, such as a trade association site. This means that Moreover has news stories that are not covered by the "regular" news sites.

Links to the stories found by Moreover are slotted into hundreds of categories so that users can go directly and easily to news stories of interest. The accounting news area at *http://w.moreover.com/accounting* is stunningly detailed and current to the nanosecond.

While Moreover news categories are broad, ranging from consumer news to sports, the business news section is especially well represented. There are 25 categories of just finance news. A search for venture capital news stories resulted in over a dozen hits from sources like the *Financial Times,* Red Herring, and the *New York Times,* all published on the day of the search. The search engine is somewhat basic, but once you do an initial search you have the opportunity to refine the search by specifying several fields including news source and market sector.

Northern Light Special Collection

www.nlresearch.com   (Exhibit 1.8)

Type: Specialty—Periodicals

Free site

> The Northern Light Special Collection is a database of business documents from more than 7,100 journals, books, magazines, newswires, and reference sources. The sources include a variety of publications, such as *American Banker, Engineering News Record, The Lancet,* PR Newswire, and ABC News Transcripts. Also available are specialty research reports from analysts at Investext and WEFA, Inc. There is no charge to search the Special Collection, but a small fee is charged to download the full text of an article. Most Special Collection documents range in price from $1 to $4 per article, with a few specialty sources, such as WEFA and Investext reports, costing more.

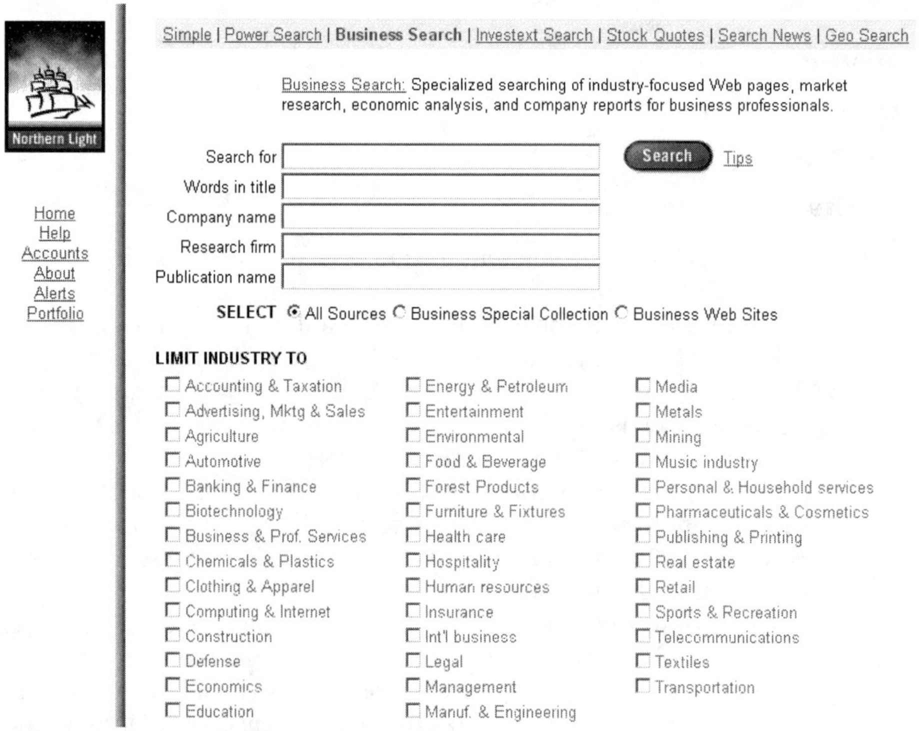

Exhibit 1.8 Northern Light: Business Search
Courtesy of Northern Light Technology, Inc.

Northern Light has a powerful search engine that supports natural language and Boolean searching. You can search by field (e.g., URL, title, publication) and use wildcards. In addition, Northern Light has set up several specific search forms tailored to different sets of sources. A Business Search form gives users the option to search only business publications. The Power Search form allows searches to be limited by language, date, or publication title. The Investext Search limits searching to the Investext investment research report collection. Similarly, the Market Research form and the WEFA form limits searching to those collections.

Northern Light also has a very good general Web search engine at *www. northernlight.com.* Particularly helpful to searchers are the Northern Light Custom Search Folders, which organize the results of your search into categories by

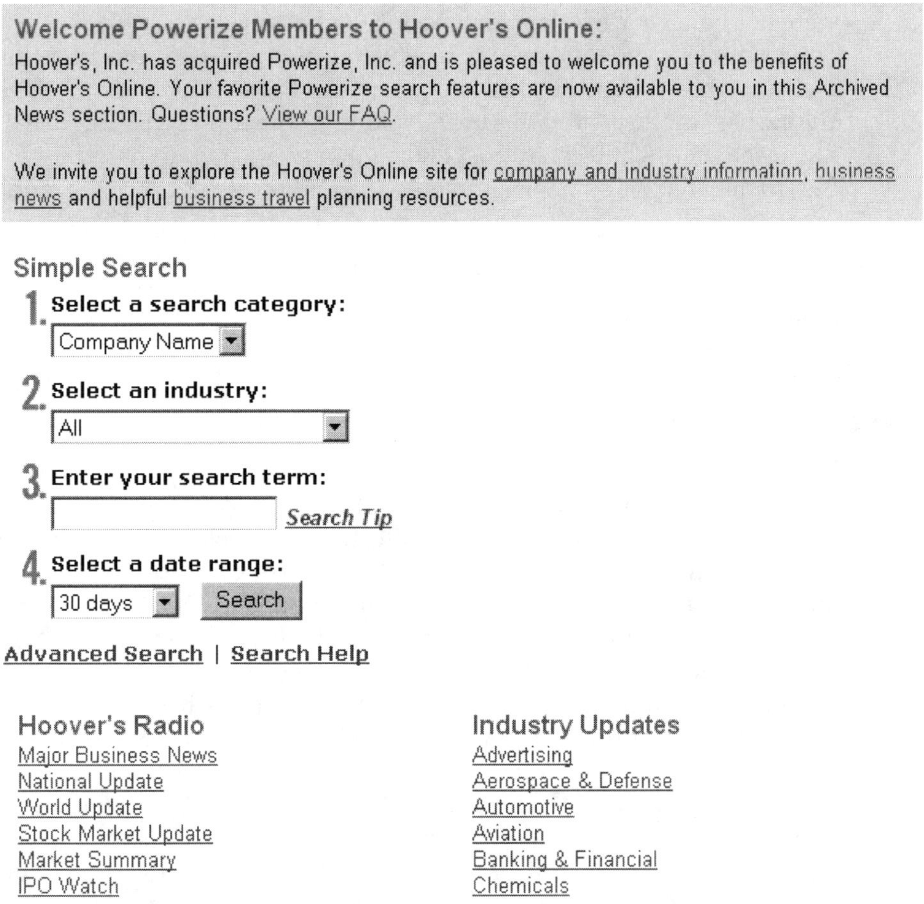

Welcome Powerize Members to Hoover's Online:

Hoover's, Inc. has acquired Powerize, Inc. and is pleased to welcome you to the benefits of Hoover's Online. Your favorite Powerize search features are now available to you in this Archived News section. Questions? View our FAQ.

We invite you to explore the Hoover's Online site for company and industry information, business news and helpful business travel planning resources.

Simple Search

1. **Select a search category:**
[Company Name ▼]

2. **Select an industry:**
[All ▼]

3. **Enter your search term:**
[　　　　　　　] *Search Tip*

4. **Select a date range:**
[30 days ▼] [Search]

Advanced Search | Search Help

Hoover's Radio
Major Business News
National Update
World Update
Stock Market Update
Market Summary
IPO Watch

Industry Updates
Advertising
Aerospace & Defense
Automotive
Aviation
Banking & Financial
Chemicals

Exhibit 1.9   Powerize/Hoover's Online

subject, type, source, and language. For example, a search on the phrase "intellectual property" generated 700,000 hits that were categorized by Northern Light into the following folders: Intellectual Property Law, Attorneys, Copyright Law, Patent & Trademark Office, World Trade Organization, and Patent Law.

Powerize

www.powerize.com   (Exhibit 1.9)

Type: Specialty—Periodicals

Free site

Powerize indexes more than 2,400 specialized industry publications. Among these publications are trade journals and industry newsletters that previously were not generally available on the Internet. Approximately one-fourth of the articles are free; the remainder are available on a pay-per-view basis for a nominal fee. The content on this site is excellent, but, unfortunately, the search engine has few advanced features, making it sometimes difficult to extract just the article you want. In August 2000, Powerize was purchased by Hoover's, Inc. To date Hoover's has maintained the Powerize URL, pricing, and format.

Yahoo!

www.yahoo.com   (Exhibit 1.10)

Type: General

Free site

Yahoo! is the grand dame of Internet search tools. Its beginning as the personal website list of two Ph.D. candidates at Stanford University in 1994 is now Silicon Valley lore. So why is Yahoo! still the self-proclaimed "leading guide in terms of traffic, advertising, household and business user reach, and one of the most recognized brands associated with the Internet"? The answer is because it is an innovative, quality site that is constantly adding new features while still meticulously maintaining its core directory site.

Yahoo!, the most general of the general search tools, has developed a number of specialty sites under the Yahoo! umbrella. Looking for investment information, detailed stock quotes and research on public companies, business news, and personal finance sites? Then check out Yahoo! Finance at *http://finance.yahoo.com.* Looking for full-text news stories and related websites for a variety of business topics, such as "Initial Public Offerings," "Electronic Commerce," and "Pharmaceutical Industry"? Then you will want Full Coverage Business at *http:// dailynews.yahoo.com/fc/Business,* where a team of editors compiles pages that link

Enter one or more symbols below. Symbol Lookup

| | Get Quotes | Basic ▼ |

View your NDB brokerage accounts on Yahoo!

Investing

Today's Markets
Market Overview NEW!, Most Actives, IPOs, Earnings, Indices, *more...*

News & Editorial
Motley Fool, TheStreet.com, Forbes, FinanceVision, *more...*

Mutual Funds
Top Performers, Prospectuses, Screener, *more...*

International
Int'l Finance Center, Indices, News, Exchange Rates

Research & Education
Splits, Up/Downgrades, Co. Index, Education Center, Glossary, *more...*

Community
Message Boards, Clubs, Chats, Net Events, Investment Challenge

Personal Finance

Banking and Bills
Bill Pay, Banking Center, PayDirect

Insurance
Auto, Life, Home & Renter's

Taxes
Online Tax Filing, Investor's Guide, Tax Estimator, *more...*

Loans
Auto Loans, Mortgages, Credit Reports

Top Business News as of 8:19pm ET

Earnings Fears Hit Internet, Chip Stocks
Stocks tumbled on Tuesday as renewed fears of slowing earnings hammered computer chip makers and worries about declining advertising spending knocked down media shares like America Online.

Intel Net Beats Expectations
Intel Corp. on Tuesday reported third-quarter earnings that topped diminished expectations as flagging sales in Europe cut into revenue at the world's largest chipmaker, which also forecast higher sales in the typically strong fourth quarter.

Market Summary   [Edit]

Nasdaq @ 4:29pm (C) Yahoo!

17-Oct 10am 12pm 2pm 4pm 6pm

Dow	10089.71	-149.09 (-1.46%)
Nasdaq	3213.96	-76.32 (-2.32%)
S&P 500	1349.97	-24.65 (-1.79%)
30-Yr Bond	5.761%	-0.052
NYSE Volume		1,167,011,000
Nasdaq Volume		1,938,427,000

Close For a while, it looked like today was going to be one of those real ugly days in the equity market... Although the major indices started on a positive note, they quickly headed south, and appeared as if they weren't going to stop as any type of bounce was being met with selling interest... That trend persisted until around 14:15 ET when the Dow, Nasdaq, and S&P bottomed out with losses of 211, 117, and 32 points respectively...
more...

FinanceVision ▭

Featured segments
- Bio-Tech Report - Lindsey Arent
- VC Report - Caleb Goddard
- New Products Report - Jay Rubin

Exhibit 1.10 Yahoo! Finance

to news sources, individual articles, and websites about particular topics. What about information on filing your taxes, with links to tax sites and tips on tax preparation? The Yahoo Tax Page at *http://taxes.yahoo.com* covers that.

In 2000, Google partnered with Yahoo! to act as Yahoo!'s default Web search engine. Outsourcing this function to Google allows Yahoo! to focus internally on its core directory and navigational guide while also having a high-quality search engine on the site.

BEST OF THE REST

Deja Usenet

www.deja.com/usenet

Type: Specialty—Discussion Groups

Free site

> The Deja Usenet search at Deja.com allows users to search the postings on hundreds of discussion forums. Everything from misc.invest.financial to alt.music.beatles is searchable. If you have not participated in (or searched) a newsgroup, you may be surprised by the nature of the content. Recent postings in one of the financial newsgroups covered the valuation of stock options in some detail, with one participant posting the entire text of an IRS private letter ruling. A newsgroup search is sometimes done in litigation in an attempt to locate postings by expert witnesses in which they espouse a view that differs from testimony.

Direct Hit

www.directhit.com

Type: General

Free site

> Direct Hit, a subsidiary of Ask Jeeves, Inc., uses proprietary technology to analyze the activity of millions of previous Internet searchers. Direct Hit uses this information to rank search results based on choices made by other searchers. Sites popular with searchers get the highest ranking. If past searchers usually skip the top listing and select the third one, that listing moves up.
>
> Direct Hit also suggests related searches. For example, if you search for the phrase "business valuation," Direct Hit will suggest related searches for "business valuation methods" and "partnership valuations."

Direct Search

http://gwis2.circ.gwu.edu/~gprice/direct.htm

Type: Specialty—Invisible Web

Free site

> Direct Search is a compilation of links to resources that contain data not easily or entirely accessible with general search tools. Maintained by a librarian at George Washington University, Direct Search takes you to all types of helpful

specialty databases. There is an eclectic selection of databases here, ranging from "Threatened Animals of the World Database," to "NASDAQ Monthly Share Volume Reports," to the "PWC Survey of Venture Capital."

Dow Jones Publications Library

www.wsj.com

Type: Specialty—Periodicals

Fee-based site

The Dow Jones Publication Library is a searchable database consisting of full-text articles from more than 6,000 trade journals and business publications including the full text of *The Wall Street Journal, Barron's,* and other exclusive Dow Jones publications. Articles can be downloaded for a small fee, but users must first have a paid subscription to the *Interactive Wall Street Journal* or *Dow Jones Interactive.*

Electric Library

www.elibrary.com

Type: Specialty—Periodicals

Fee-based site

The Electric Library site allows users to search an extensive full-text collection of current and archival information. Not only does the Electric Library allow searching of periodicals such as magazines, specialized journals, newspapers, and reference works, but users have access to thousands of TV and radio transcripts, photographs, and maps. Searching is free, but you cannot purchase just a single article from the Electric Library, as you can from other periodical indexes reviewed here. The bad news is that you must purchase a subscription, because only registered subscribers can download documents. The good news is that an annual subscription that will allow you to download unlimited articles is only $59.95.

FinancialFind

www.financialfind.com

Type: Specialty—Financial

Free site

> FinancialFind was developed by Goinvest.com in partnership with Microsoft Consulting Services to provide Yahoo!-type category listings covering only financial topics. FinancialFind searches a variety of business-only sites, such as *Forbes* and other financial publications, Morningstar, and investment newswires. FinancialFind supports a number of advanced search features including Boolean searching and wildcards.

FindArticles

www.findarticles.com

Type: Specialty—Periodicals

Free site

> FindArticles, a joint project of Gale Group and Looksmart, has a database of full-text articles on a range of topics not limited to business or financial matters. Searches can be carried out on the full database, on selected specific subject areas, or within a particular magazine.
>
> Articles are drawn from approximately 300 magazines and journals. While that is far fewer sources than similar services from Northern Light and Powerize, unlike its competitors, all the articles on FindArticles can be downloaded at no charge.

International Affairs

www.internationalaffairs.com

Type: Specialty—Global information

Free site

> The International Affairs site is product of Oxford Analytica, a political and economic news analysis organization that draws from a network of professors at Oxford and other universities in more than 100 countries. From the International Affairs home page you can search by country name for detailed information on that country or pick from a directory of topics covering politics, economics, international relations, and industry. The site includes a directory of political science departments at leading universities, economic think tanks, strategic studies institutes, and official websites of governments and international institutions, newswires, and newspapers.

CHAPTER 2

Economic Research

Eva M. Lang

The Internet is a rich source of economic statistics. Both government and private industry delight in measuring every component of modern industrial production and turning those measurements into statistics. The sites discussed in this chapter include both government- and private industry–sponsored repositories for those statistics.

Many of the sites discussed contain the same core statistical information. However, there is significant variation when it comes to the scope of the statistics presented, the presentation and output options, and the extent of value-added features such as analysis, discussion, and interpretation. Sites profiled here range from those offering only raw statistical data to those offering the detailed analyses of the some of the largest economic data services in the world.

All sites are presented in alphabetical order. The sites listed in the "First and Foremost" section of this chapter are those that the authors have found to be reliable, well organized, and rich sources of information. Sites offering all or part of the data for free are considered more desirable than sites offering similar data for a fee. "Best of the Rest" sites may focus on a niche area, be fee only, or have limited navigation and output features.

If you are doing regular economic research, we urge you to "test drive" a number of the sites to find the format that works best for you. Some sites allow data to be downloaded into an Excel spreadsheet while others present the data only in a plain text format. Your needs will dictate which site to choose among those with similar data.

Be sure that you are using the information obtained from a site in a manner consistent with the user guidelines. Some companies restrict the commercial use of data obtained from their sites.

Following are economic research tips:

- Take time to plan your approach to obtaining economic data. Identify the type of data you are seeking before you start searching the sites. If you are looking for just a single statistic—for example, U.S. housing starts for 1999 or the prime rate on December 18, 2000—a statistical depository like the FRED database at the Federal Reserve Bank of St. Louis is a good starting point. But if you are looking for analysis, you may want to explore the offerings of the economics departments of money center banks. The major business publications—*Forbes, Fortune, Business Week*—also cover economic developments, and a check of their websites or a periodical database such as Powerize.com may produce an article on exactly the economic topic you seek.

- If you are looking for information on local or regional economic conditions, consider searching the articles in a local newspaper or business journal. Often, area business journals run articles about important economic developments. At year end, most do a special "looking back at events in our area in the past year" article. To find a listing of local newspapers, many of which have their own websites, check a media list, such as the American Journalism Review (AJR) Newslink at *http://ajr.newslink.org.* This site links to hundreds of local newspapers and even includes listings of "alternative" and campus papers. The AJR section on business news-papers, *http://ajr.newslink. org/biznews.html,* links to business journals in many U.S. cities.

- Another option for local information is the chamber of commerce, but keep a skeptical eye out for boosterism! The information available from chambers of commerce varies widely, and the quality of the material available is not necessarily directly related to the size of the area. The U.S. Chamber of Commerce site at *www.uschamber.com* has a directory of chambers by state with links to the local chamber website.

FIRST AND FOREMOST

American FactFinder

http://factfinder.census.gov   (Exhibit 2.1)

Free site

American FactFinder is an interactive website developed by the U.S. Census Bureau. Users can browse the Bureau's data warehouse to search, view, print, and download reports and tables to come up with their own customized statistics. American FactFinder will be the Census Bureau's primary vehicle for distributing the 2000 Census of Population and Housing.

The Bureau plans to cut back significantly on the number of printed reports it issues. In 1990 the Bureau published five major reports for the 1990 Census with hundreds of tables for each state. For the 2000 census, it will produce one basic report with 80 summary tables and will eliminate printed reports on metropolitan areas, urban areas, congressional districts, and census tracts. All this census data will be available on American FactFinder.

What can you expect to find?

- Statistical demographic data
- Community profiles showing social, economic, or housing characteristics for states, cities, counties, and congressional districts
- Population and housing data from the official U.S. Census and American Community Survey
- Detailed maps showing the geographic patterns in statistical data
- Industry data from the current Economic Census

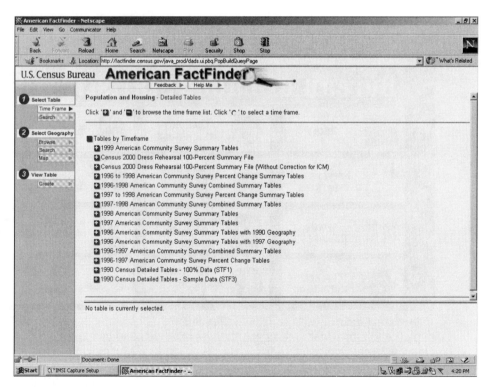

Exhibit 2.1   American FactFinder

Bureau of Labor Statistics

http://stats.bls.gov   (Exhibit 2.2)

Free site

The Bureau of Labor Statistics (BLS) site is the major repository of employment statistics on the Internet. This site is filled with hundreds of pages of statistics and publications. As a navigation aid, the BLS has segregated some statistics into the "Most Requested Series" section—*http://stats.bls.gov/top20.html.* This section includes civilian labor force and unemployment statistics along with productivity measures and consumer price index data. News releases covering all the statistics collected by the Bureau of Labor Statistics are accessible at *http://stats.bls.gov/newsrels.htm.*

Regional employment statistics are located at *http://stats.bls.gov/regnhome.htm.* BLS publications are also accessible on this site. Keyword-searchable indexes of the current *Occupational Outlook Handbook* (*http://stats.bls.gov/ocohome.htm*) and *Occupational Outlook Quarterly* (*http://stats.bls.gov/opub/ooq/ooqhome.htm*) are also available.

Data | Economy at a Glance | Keyword Search of BLS Web Pages
Surveys & Programs | Publications & Research Papers | Regional Information
News Releases | Occupational Outlook Handbook | K-12 Educational Resources
Contact Information | Mission, Management & Jobs | What's New

Exhibit 2.2   Bureau of Labor Statistics

What can you expect to find?

- Virtually any statistic related to employment in the United States as well as foreign labor statistics and international price indices
- Publications including *BLS Bulletins, Issues in Labor Statistics, National Compensation Survey, Occupational Outlook Handbook,* the *Monthly Labor Review, Compensation and Working Conditions, Employment and Earnings,* and the *Consumer Price Index* (CPI) and *Producer Price Index* (PPI) Detailed Reports
- Research papers, statistical papers, and economic working papers
- The National Compensation Survey providing information on the average hourly earnings by occupation in 150 cities and counties

Dismal Scientist

www.dismal.com   (Exhibit 2.3)

Free and Fee-based site

The Dismal Scientist site is a great mix of interesting and timely articles on economic topics as well as detailed economic statistics. The authors pull off a major coup by actually making the articles fun to read. Many of the articles use popular culture as a launching point for a discussion of an economic concept. Among the more interesting topics have been "Tony Soprano Meets the Computer Age" (the role of the mafia in computer fraud), "Who Wants to Marry an Economist?" (proposals to restructure the tax system to eliminate the marriage tax), "Risk Sharing with Jennifer Lopez" (asymmetries in the insurance market), and "Something to W(h)ine About" (unfair and inconsistent state laws governing alcohol sales).

In addition to the articles, the site has a wealth of more prosaic economic information. The data section contains forecasts for numerous data series on the national level as well as state-level data and rankings and data on over 250 metropolitan areas. There is also an up-to-date section on the current economic releases from all the major government agencies and a special area for academicians.

What about the name? What exactly is Dismal Science? According to the site's authors, "The name Dismal Scientist comes from the term 'dismal science,' which has long been associated with economics and originated in the writings of the Scottish essayist and historian Thomas Carlyle. He coined the term while referring to Thomas Malthus and his belief that exponential population growth and linear food supply growth would result in worldwide famine. Since then, economics has also been referred to as the dismal science because of the general notion of diminishing marginal returns."

What can you expect to find?

- Hundreds of interesting articles on every aspect of the economy dating back to 1997
- A "Zip Code Economic Profile" that allows users to enter a zip code to generate a report of economic indicators for a metropolitian area
- Forecasts of more than 150 data series covering the U.S. economy

There are two other sites in the Dismal Science family that you will want to check out:

- FreeLunch (*www.FreeLunch.com*). FreeLunch claims to provide users with more than 1 million economic and financial data series. Numbers on everything from housing starts to international trade statistics can be downloaded directly into Microsoft Excel.
- Research@Economy.com (*www.economy.com/research*). This site sells reports on a variety of economic, industrial, and financial topics. Reports include "Occupation Forecast Tables" that include detailed historical and forecast reports for 100 occupations in 315 metropolitan areas and all states. The

HOME	ECONOMIC RELEASES	DATA	THOUGHTS	ACADEMICS	TOOLKIT	ABOUT

Browse Dismal.com: Quick Find   Companion

Other Categories
- Demographics
- Labor
- Income
- Real Estate

Associated Metros
- Chattanooga
- Clarksville Hopkinsville
- Jackson
- Johnson City Kingsport Bristol
- Knoxville
- Nashville

Southeast
- Alabama
- Arkansas
- Florida
- Georgia
- Kentucky
- Louisiana
- Mississippi

Memphis TN-AR-MS MSA by Vital Statistics Categories
◁ Tennessee by Vital Statistics Categories

Category	Value	Rank	Date	Source*
Pop. Density, (#/Sq. Mile)	335.8	88	1990	BOC: PoE
Total Population, (000s)	1,105.1	56	1999	BOC: PoE
Net Migration, (000s)	3.9	65	1999	BOC: PoE
Nonfarm Employment, (000s)	595.9	54	Aug-00	BLS
% Chg. Year Ago	1.7	126	Aug-00	BLS
Unemployment Rate, (%)	3.7	157	Jul-00	BLS: HdE
Labor Force, (000s)	572.0	56	Jul-00	BLS: HdE
% Chg. Year Ago	2.0	129	Jul-00	BLS: HdE
Total Personal Income, (Mil $)	30,053.3	55	1998	BEA
Annual % Chg.	7.3	39	1998	BEA
Per Capita Income, ($)	27,511.0	84	1998	BEA
Annual % Chg.	6.3	26	1998	BEA
Median Household Income, ($)	26,899.0	180	1989	BOC: DeC
Annualized 10 Year % Chg.	5.9	119	1989	BOC: DeC
Median Home Price, (Ths.$, SA)	113.1	146	00Q2	NAR; BOC
% Chg. Year Ago	1.8	270	00Q2	NAR; BOC

Additional Information Available at Economy.com

For a comprehensive report on the Memphis TN-AR-MS MSA economy, including detailed forecast and analysis, click here.

Exhibit 2.3   Memphis MSA Data—Dismal Scientist

"Metropolitan Area Reports" are short analyses and forecasts of the local economies of U.S. metropolitan areas.

One URL (*www.economy.com*) provides the gateway to all the sites related to the Dismal Scientist.

Economagic

www.Economagic.com   (Exhibit 2.4)

Free site

The development of the Economagic site is a typical Internet success story. Like many sites, it started modestly enough as a repository of data collected for students. Ted Bos, a University of Alabama at Birmingham economics professor, originally designed Economagic to give students taking his Applied Forecasting class easy access to economic information. The collection grew to more than 100,000 data files.

Economagic gathers and manipulates statistics from government agencies in the United States, Canada, and Japan as well as trade associations and pri-

Economagic.com: Economic Time Series Page

Browse Data Titles | Books | Charts | Excel | Reports | Search | Maps & Movies | Help | About | Contact Us
Subscriber Login | Subscription Info | Turn Advanced Features On | Change Defaults | Disclaimer

Get any Economagic data in a spreadsheet
Click here to find out more   Economagic.com

Browse Data Collections
Over 100,000 data files, with charts and excel files for each

Collection	• Most Requested Series
Browse by Region	• Data by State: including DC, Puerto Rico, and Virgin Is.
Browse by Source	• **U.S. Government**

- **U.S. Government**
  - **Federal Reserve, Board of Governors**
    - Interest Rates: 40 series
    - Consumer Credit: 40+ series
    - Senior Loan Officer Opinion Survey: 10 series
    - Industrial Production, Capacity, Utilization and Electric Power Use: 400+ series
  - Federal Reserve, St. Louis: 350+ series
  - Federal Reserve, Dallas: 150+ series
  - Federal Reserve, New York: Daily Foreign Exchange: 34 series
  - Federal Reserve, Chicago: House Sales, Starts, Permits: 15 series
  - Federal Reserve, Philadelphia: Third Federal Reserve District, *Business Outlook Survey*
  - **Census Bureau**
    - Retail Sales by Kind of Business: 80+ series
    - Building Permits by Region, State, and Metro Areas: 4,000+ series
  - **Bureau of Labor Statistics**
    - US Civilian Labor Force: 22,000+ series

Exhibit 2.4   Economagic.com: Economic Time Series Page

vate companies. The data can be displayed as plain numbers, in charts, or in spreadsheets, where it can be analyzed and downloaded.

Most of the data on Economagic is available at no charge, but some features, such as forecasting, are available only to subscribers. Much of the free data, such as employment statistics from the Bureau of Labor Statistics, interest rates from the Federal Reserve System, and building permit data from the Census Bureau, are available on other sites discussed in this chapter. The advantages of the Economagic site are easy access to all the statistics on a single site, the capability to view them in multiple formats, and the option to download directly into a spreadsheet.

What can you expect to find?

- Statistics only in graphical or numeric formats
- Data from the Federal Reserve System, Department of Commerce, Bureau of Labor Statistics, Census Bureau, Bank of Canada, and Bank of Japan
- Capability to view data by state; for example, there are more than 1,500 statistics for local and statewide information in Florida
- Interactive charts of data series

The *Economic Report of the President*

http://w3.access.gpo.gov/eop   (Exhibit 2.5)

Free site

The Council of Economic Advisers is responsible for producing the annual *Economic Report of the President*. This 400+ page document is published each February by the Government Printing Office. Approximately 75 percent of the report is devoted to detailed analyses of economic conditions. Samples of the chapter titles in the 1999 edition are "Macroeconomic Policy and Performance," "Benefits of a Strong Labor Market," and "Capital Flows in the Global Economy."

The real treasure in the *Economic Report of the President* lies in the appendix to the report, the "Statistical Tables Relating to Income, Employment, and Production." It is these 112 tables that will make the heart of any statistician beat faster. The tables cover all aspects of the economy from income to population to corporate profits to agriculture. Historical data is presented so trends can be plotted over the last 40 or 50 years. Most of the data is aggregated annually, and for some statistics more recent data is presented monthly or quarterly. For example, you can look up bond yields dating back to 1929. A searchable index

- Economic Report of the President (PDF, size: 5 MB)

    You can **download** the entire report from **previous years** in PDF format (1995-forward) as well as access the statistical tables from Appendix B as spreadsheet files (1997-forward) by clicking here.

Exhibit 2.5 The Economic Report of the President

of the *Economic Report of the President* for each year since 1995 is available on the Government Printing Office site.

What can you expect to find?

- 125 pages of statistical tables relating to income, employment, and production in the United States from the current report in Adobe PDF format and in a spreadsheet format
- Full text of all *Economic Reports of the President* since 1995
- The Changing America Report: Documents differences in economic well-being for various racial and ethnic groups and traces the evolution of such differences over the past several decades

Federal Reserve District Banks

www.federalreserve.gov/otherfrb.htm   (Exhibit 2.6)

Free site

The Federal Reserve System site includes a map of all 12 Federal Reserve Banks (FRBs) with links to each bank's website. The amount and accessibility of information varies among FRB websites because there is no standard format for the data. Typically, you will find background information on each FRB, along with information on the workings of the Fed, publications produced, economic analysis sources, and regional economic data.

To get a sense of the scope of the data available in the Federal Reserve System, visit the *Publication Information Catalog* at *http://app.ny.frb.org/cfpicnic/main.cfm* or the *Fed in Print* at *www.frbsf.org/publications/fedinprint/index.html*. These two publications are hosted by the New York and San Francisco FRBs, respectively, but catalog data is available throughout the system. The main Federal Reserve System website, *www.bog.frb.fed.us*, does not offer a comprehensive catalog of resources but refers users to these two sites. The *Publication Information Catalog* is a comprehensive guide to all online, printed, and audio/visual materials available from the Federal Reserve. The *Fed in Print* publication is a searchable index to Federal Reserve Economic Research.

Several of the FRBs maintain specialized databases that merit mention:

- FRB Philadelphia publishes the Livingston Survey, the oldest continuous survey of economists' expectations, and the Survey of Professional

The Federal Reserve Board

The Twelve Federal Reserve Districts

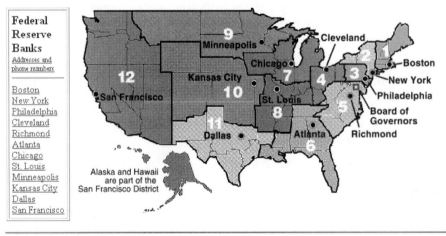

Exhibit 2.6   The Federal Reserve: The Twelve Federal Reserve Districts

Forecasters, a quarterly survey of macroeconomic forecasts. Data generated by the Livingston Survey and the Survey of Professional Forecasters is available at *www.phil.frb.org*.

- FRB St. Louis is home to the FRED (Federal Reserve Economic Data) database of economic statistics at *www.stls.frb.org/fred*. The extensive FRED database covers hundreds of national and regional economic statistics, from housing starts, to interest rates, to unemployment rates. Many of the statistics date back 40 years or more. FRED is a great resource for historical interest rates. On FRED's interest rate page at *www.stls.frb.org/fred/data/ irates.html* you can find a listing of a variety of rates (prime rate, Fed funds rate, 20-Year Treasury Constant Maturity Rate, and 39 other rates), some dating back to 1914.

Some of the FRBs specialize in the study of economic conditions in a specific geographic area.

- The FRB San Francisco created the Center for Pacific Basin Monetary and Economic Studies in 1990. The Pacific Basin program promotes cooperation among central banks in the region and enhances public understanding of major Pacific Basin economic policy issues. Data on the center is available at *www.frbsf.org/economics/pbc/index.html*.

- Two of the FRBs, Dallas and Atlanta, focus on the economy of Latin America. In 1992 the FRB Dallas established a Center for Latin American Economics to promote public understanding of Latin American economic policy issues and to serve as a clearinghouse for information on Latin America. Access to the center is on the FRB Dallas website at *www.dallasfed.org*. In 1994 the FRB Atlanta launched the Latin American Research Group at *www.frbatlanta.org/econ_rd/larg/index.htm* to study economic, financial, and political developments in Latin America and the Caribbean.

- FRB Kansas City established the Center for the Study of Rural America in 1999, and its website is at *www.kc.frb.org/RuralCenter/RuralMain.htm*. The center collects statistics on rural economic and agricultural conditions and publishes the Main Street Economist, a newsletter featuring commentary on the rural economy.

What can you expect to find?

- Regional demographic statistics and economic indicators
- Newsletters with interesting articles on regional economic growth

- In-dept economic research including working papers and conference information
- Detailed information on banks including financial statements and merger data. (Chicago Fed at *www.chicagofed.org*)

Federal Reserve System

www.federalreserve.gov/rnd.htm   (Exhibit 2.7)

Free site

The Federal Reserve System collects and disseminates a variety of monetary statistics, including interest rates, money supply, and foreign exchange rates. Through its network of 12 Federal Reserve District Banks, the Fed also provides detailed regional economic analyses.

In the "Research and Data" section of the Federal Reserve site, you will find links to current and historical monetary statistics. The frequency of releases of new statistics varies. Some items, such as selected interest rates and commercial paper yields, are released daily and then aggregated in weekly and quarterly documents. Banking statistics, such as data on minority-owned banks and delinquency rates on loans, are published quarterly. The Federal Reserve also publishes a number of surveys, studies, reports, and working papers that are also available on the site.

Eight times a year, the Fed publishes a compilation of reports on economic conditions in each of the 12 Federal Reserve Bank districts. In this publication, known as the *Beige Book,* the Fed gathers anecdotal information on current economic conditions in each district from interviews with key business contacts, economists, market experts, and other sources. Copies of the *Beige Book,* starting with the October 1996 issue, are available at *www.federalreserve.gov/FOMC/ BeigeBook/2000.* A searchable index of the *Beige Book* series beginning with the first issue in 1970 is available from the Federal Reserve Bank of Minneapolis at *http://minneapolisfed.org/bb.*

What can you expect to find?

- Statistics on banking, interest rates, and money supplies and articles relating to the U.S. banking system and monetary policy
- Current and historical coverage of the 36 selected interest rates published in the *H.15 Interest Rate Release*
- Data on consumer credit and the household debt-service burden
- Exchange rates for the major industrialized countries dating to the early 1970s

The Federal Reserve Board

Home
General Information
Press Releases
Testimony and Speeches
Monetary Policy
Banking System
Regulation and Supervision
Research and Data
Consumer Information
Community Affairs
Reporting Forms
Publications
Career Opportunities

Research and Data

- **Statistics: Releases and Historical Data**
  Daily, weekly, monthly, quarterly, and annual, including commercial paper, loan charge-offs, and medium term notes
- **Surveys and Reports**
  Includes the senior loan officer survey, the survey on small business finances, and the survey of consumer finances
- **Staff Studies**
  A series of pubished studies covering a wide range of economic and financial subjects.
- **Working Papers**
  Preliminary discussion papers in domestic and international topics, occasional staff studies, and links to other working papers sites
- **Federal Reserve Bulletin Articles**
  Reports and analysis on economic developments, regulatory issues and new data

FOIA | FAQ | Search | Site Map | Web Publication Schedule | What's New

Exhibit 2.7 The Federal Reserve Board: Research and Data

- Articles from the *Federal Reserve Bulletin,* a monthly print publication, analyzing economic developments and discussing bank regulatory issues
- From the *Beige Book,* more than 30 pages of economic discussion and analysis by Federal Reserve district

FedStats

www.fedstats.gov   (Exhibit 2.8)

Free site

Much more than economic statistics, this site is a compendium of a wide variety of links to statistics collected by more than 70 agencies of the United States Federal Government. FedStats is not a comprehensive collection of every statistic available from every agency, but it does pull together hundreds of statistics into one easy-to-search site.

Many of the statistical series focus on health, safety, and education, but there is also a number of economic and demographic statistics. These statistics include labor data from the Bureau of Labor Statistics, the Employment Standards Administration, and the Employment and Training Administration. Economic statistics are collected from the Census Bureau, the Department of Commerce, the Economics and Statistics Administration, the U.S. Army Corps of Engineers, and the Small Business Administration.

Unlike sites such as Economagic or EconData that take government-issued statistics and recast them, FedStats merely links to the data on the sites of the respective government agency.

What can you expect to find?

- Links to statistical data from more than 70 government agencies
- Descriptions of all the U.S. Government agencies that report statistics and the type of statistics they report

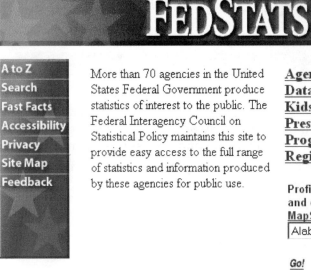

Exhibit 2.8   FedStats

- U.S. Waterway Monthly Tonnage Indicators from the U.S. Corps of Engineers

- Food consumption statistics from the Agricultural Research Service

- Population estimates from the Census Bureau

Money Center Banks—Economic Departments

Free sites

When asked why he robbed banks, Willie Sutton replied "That's where the money is." Banks are also "where the data is." It stands to reason that bankers who need access to economic statistics to assist in decision making would want to track and analyze economic data. In the United States, large regional banks, referred to as money center banks, have traditionally maintained economic departments. The increasing pace of bank merger activity in the 1990s reduced the number of banks with economics departments (let us pause for a moment to mourn the loss of the excellent economics department at First Interstate), but there are still a few banks producing generally high-quality economic analyses. We recommend the economics departments at three money center banks, Bank of America, Bank One, and First Union, which have great websites that allow you to download free information. The websites of all three of these banks will give you access to thoughtful and well-written economic overviews of national (and sometimes regional) conditions.

Bank of America
*http://corp.bankofamerica.com/research/e_economic_
analysis_research.html*

The "Economic Analysis and Research" section of the Bank of America website provides insightful overviews of national economic conditions. The monthly *Economic & Financial Perspectives* publication, downloadable in Adobe PDF format, is a four- to six-page discussion by Bank of America's chief economists of current economic conditions. A sampling of articles from *Economic & Financial Perspectives* includes such titles as "An Economic Soft-Landing: Characteristics and Financial Market Responses," "Rising Wages & Inflation," "The U.S. Economy, the Fed and the Financial Markets," and "Federal Reserve Policy and Financial Market Performance During Presidential Election Years: Myths and Reality."

What can you expect to find?

- U.S. Economic Calendar: "A weekly publication featuring U.S. economic indicators, BAC forecasts and commentary from the domestic economic team."

- Economic Briefs: "Succinct reports provided by the Office of the Chief Economist on the key issues influencing the economy and financial markets."
- Economic & Financial Perspectives: "Detailed as well as more comprehensive monthly reports on key issues, as prepared by the Office of the Chief Economist."
- U.S. Economic Indicators: "Market commentary on recently released economic reports."

While visiting the Bank of America site, you may want to check out the "Industry Focus" section. Here you will find publications related to the Food and Agribusiness industry, including *Agribusiness Quarterly, Protein Products Quarterly, Grocery Wholesaling Industry Review and Outlook,* and *Food Processing & Distribution Quarterly.*

Bank One
www.bankone.com/commercial/research/economics

The Bank One Corporate Economics Group is staffed by three full-time economists who gather economic data and publish a number of weekly and monthly economic and industry updates. Start with the "Outlook-at-a-Glance," the weekly economic forecast. It is a six-page Adobe PDF publication that covers the business cycle outlook, inflation, monetary policy, the stock and bond markets, international issues, labor, housing, transportation, and energy as well as a brief regional roundup.

What can you expect to find?

- Outlook-at-a-Glance: "A weekly summary of the Bank One economic forecast."
- One View: "A monthly update on economic conditions in the U.S. and key regional economies."
- Housing Watch: A weekly analysis and forecast of the housing market.
- Auto Watch: "A weekly analysis and forecast of the auto industry."
- WorldWatch: "A weekly analysis and forecast of major U.S. trading partners."

The Corporate Economics Group section of the Bank One website also contains a section called "Useful Data." Here you can find historical interest rates and inflation information for the past ten years.

The Corporate Economics Group has not cornered the market on great research at Bank One. The Bank One Capital Markets Group has dozens of publications containing interest rate forecasts, international market analyses and market summaries. See *www.fcnbd.com/cor/fccm/Research_Root/guide/publications.html* for a list of publications offered by Bank One Capital Markets.

First Union
www.firstunion.com/econews (Exhibit 2.9)

The Economics Group of First Union, headquartered in Charlotte, North Carolina, covers both the U.S. and the southeastern regional economy. Their primary publication is the five-page "Monthly Economic Outlook" that is downloadable from the website in Adobe PDF format. Each month the First Union economists present an overview of both the U.S. and international economy with a forecast of economic indicators.

Exhibit 2.9 First Union's Economic Information

What can you expect to find?

- Monthly Economic Outlook: a monthly discussion of the state of the U.S. and international economy
- Weekly Economic & Financial Commentary: a discussion of recently released economic indicators along with the interest rate watch and a topic of the week
- Southeast Regional Economic Review: a state-by-state analysis of current and projected economic conditions

National Bureau of Economic Research

www.nber.org   (Exhibit 2.10)

Free and Fee-based site

To see a cross-section of the economic research work being done by a variety of universities, visit the National Bureau of Economic Research (NBER) website. NBER is a private, nonprofit, nonpartisan organization bringing together research conducted by more than 500 university professors in the United States. Clearly, some of the brightest minds in the country are contributing to the development of economic theory at NBER. They are especially proud that 10 of the 29 American Nobel Prize winners in Economics and three of the past chairs of the President's Council of Economic Advisers have been researchers at the NBER.

Publications produced by the NBER and available from the website include working papers, the *NBER Digest,* and the *NBER Reporter.* Working papers published after 1994 are available on the site for a nominal charge. Users can access a searchable index of the working papers for free at *http://papers.nber.org/papers.html.* Dozens of new papers are issued each month that cover a variety of topics, with titles such as:

- "Cornucopia: The Pace of Economic Growth in the Twentieth Century"
- "Asset Pricing at the Millennium"
- "Compensation in the Nonprofit Sector"
- "Medical Liability, Managed Care, and Defensive Medicine"

The *NBER Digest* is a monthly publication that summarizes recent and newsworthy *NBER Working Papers.* The summaries are written by professional journalists for a nontechnical audience. The *NBER Digest* is available on the site at *www.nber.org/digest.*

The *NBER Reporter* covers the workings of the NBER on a quarterly basis. Each issue includes a full list of all new working papers along with coverage of NBER conferences and other research activities. The *NBER Reporter* is available online at *www.nber.org/reporter*.

For readers who are interested in other academic resources for economics study, a list of all university economics departments in the United States is available at *http://price.bus.okstate.edu/econdept.html*.

What can you expect to find?

- The Macrohistory database covering all aspects of the pre-WWI and inter-war economies, including production, construction, employment, money, prices, asset market transactions, foreign trade, and government activity (The index alone is 336 pages)
- Searchable catalog of books dating to the 1920s published by NBER
- Listing of all NBER studies cited in articles in the business and financial press
- Working papers, articles, and conferences on economic topics

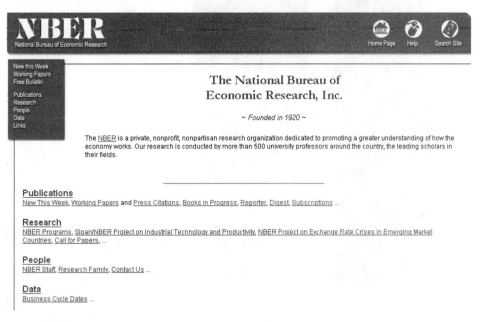

Exhibit 2.10   National Bureau of Economic Research

Report of the Council of Economic Advisers to Congress

www.access.gpo.gov/congress/cong002.html   (Exhibit 2.11)

Free site

Each month the Council of Economic Advisers prepares a report of economic statistics for Congress. Reports dating back to April 1995 are available on this site. These reports are typically about 40 pages long and contain only tables and graphs. All the major economic indicators, such as gross domestic product, income measures, price indices, employment data, credit market data, and some international statistics, are included.

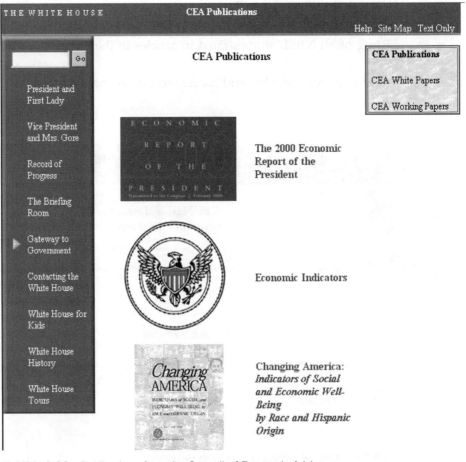

Exhibit 2.11 Publications from the Council of Economic Advisers

What can you expect to find?

- Statistical tables and graphs of major economic indicators
- Interest rates and bond yields for the last 10 years
- New private housing and vacancy rates
- New construction activity
- Unemployment rates and labor statistics
- Business sales and inventories
- Personal income statistics

U.S. Census Bureau

www.census.gov   (Exhibit 2.12)

Free site

Many people may think the Census Bureau is limited to collecting and disseminating information about the U.S. population every 10 years. However, the population data collected, while extensive, is only a part of the work of the Census Bureau. The Bureau also conducts the lesser-known, but no less important, Economic Censuses and Census of Governments. These surveys are the cornerstones of U.S. economic statistics, providing five-year benchmarks on businesses, industries, and nonfederal governments. The Economic Census covers:

- Retail and wholesale trade and selected service industries
- Construction activity, such as housing permits and starts, the values of new construction, residential alterations and repairs, and quarterly price indices for new, single-family houses
- Quantities and values of industrial output and manufacturing activities; shipments, inventories, and orders; capital expenditure information
- Foreign trade, including imports, exports, and trade monitoring
- State and local government activities

The Bureau also maintains a section on its website devoted to current economic indicators. The Economics Briefing Room at *www.census.gov/cgi-bin/ briefroom/BriefRm* has collected the major current economic indicators on a single page. Each indicator is displayed with a brief description of the indicator, a thumbnail version of a chart of the indicator over time, and comparative information.

For those looking for in-depth information not available to the general public, the Census Bureau established the Center for Economic Studies (CES) at *www.census.gov/cecon/www/ceshome.html.* The CES serves researchers and policymakers in government, academia, and business who need access to Census Bureau records for model-based statistical research. Working papers, with titles such as "Bank Loans as Predictors of Small Business Start-up Survival," are downloadable from the CES at *www.census.gov/cecon/www/papers.html.*

What can you expect to find?

- Statistical data, including detailed information from the 1990 U.S. Census in the areas of population, housing, and income
- Current population estimates for U.S. cities, counties/parishes, and states

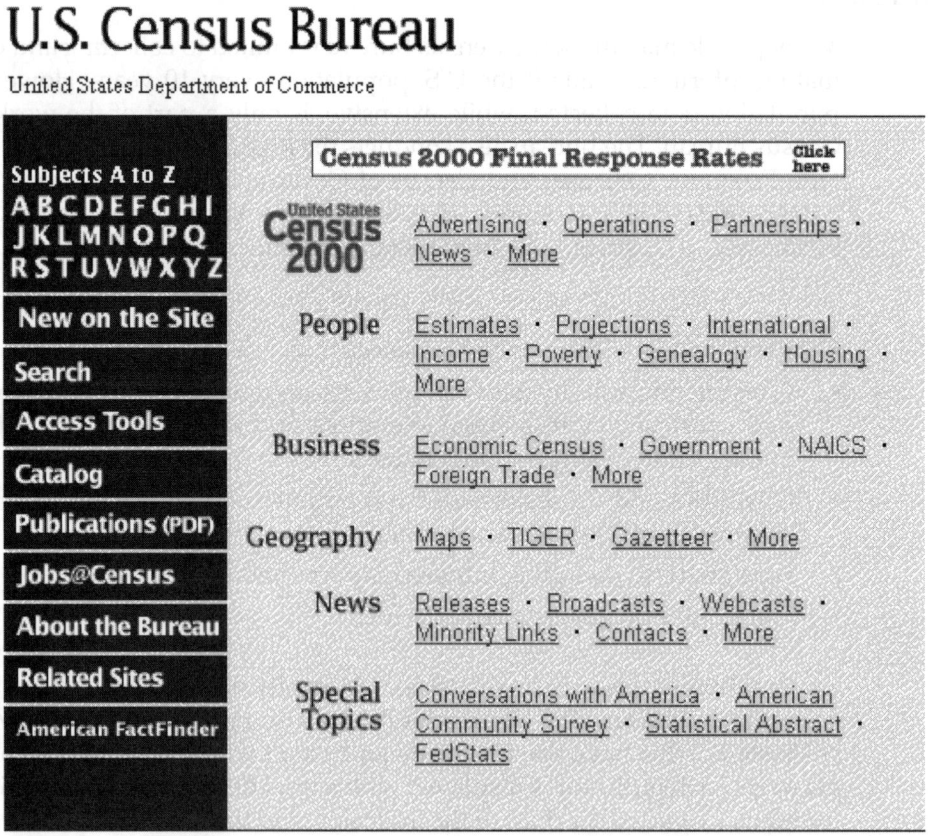

U.S. Census Bureau

United States Department of Commerce

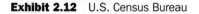

Census 2000 Final Response Rates ^{Click here}

Subjects A to Z
A B C D E F G H I
J K L M N O P Q
R S T U V W X Y Z

New on the Site

Search

Access Tools

Catalog

Publications (PDF)

Jobs@Census

About the Bureau

Related Sites

American FactFinder

United States **Census 2000**
Advertising · Operations · Partnerships · News · More

People   Estimates · Projections · International · Income · Poverty · Genealogy · Housing · More

Business   Economic Census · Government · NAICS · Foreign Trade · More

Geography   Maps · TIGER · Gazetteer · More

News   Releases · Broadcasts · Webcasts · Minority Links · Contacts · More

Special Topics   Conversations with America · American Community Survey · Statistical Abstract · FedStats

Exhibit 2.12   U.S. Census Bureau

- Detailed reports from the Economic Census covering business and industry statistics
- Detailed press releases on current economic indicators

Yardeni's Economics Network

www.yardeni.com   (Exhibit 2.13)

Free site

Dr. Ed Yardeni is the Chief Global Economist and Investment Strategist of Deutsche Bank Securities in New York. He has put together a great site built around the publications and topical studies that he writes for Deutsche Bank. His interest in the effects of both demographics and technology on the economy is evident in his downloadable papers and charts on the movement of the baby boomer generation through the economy and on the effects of the Internet and technology on the "new" economy.

Dr. Yardeni attracted media attention in the late 1990s with his warnings about the potential problems related to the Y2K bug. Many believe his efforts to bring attention to the Y2K bug as early as 1997 were one reason why action was taken in time to prevent problems. Visitors to Dr. Yardeni's website in the

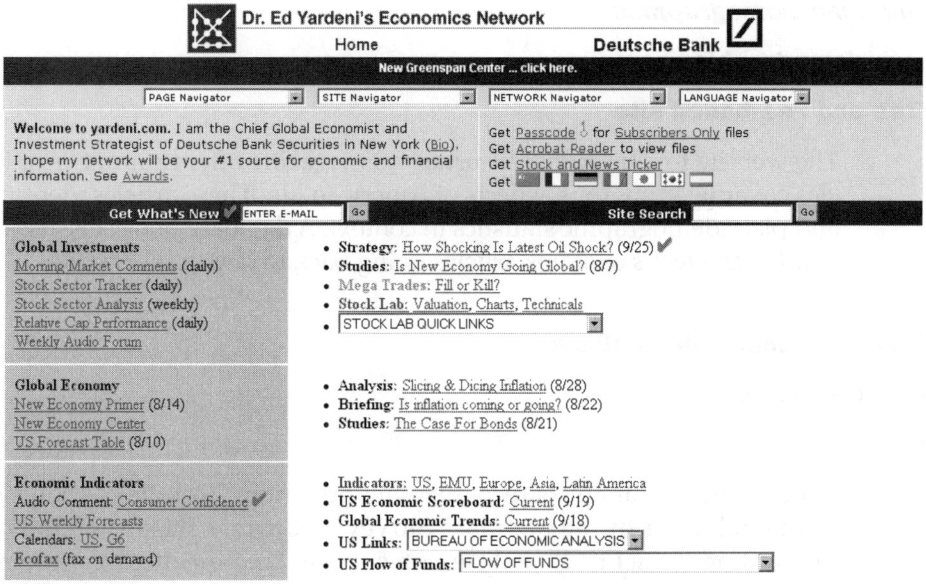

Exhibit 2.13   Dr. Ed Yardeni's Economics Network

late 1990s found a plethora of articles and information about the potential Y2K problem. Since January 1, 2000, Dr. Yardeni's focus had shifted back to basic issues of economic and market growth.

On the site, users can find detailed information on the U.S. and global markets, economic indicators, articles, trends and forecasts, and lots of charts. Access to some of the most current data is restricted to customers of Deutsche Bank Securities, but most of the data is free to the public.

What can you expect to find?

- Daily morning market commentary
- Topical studies such as the 12-page "Age Wave Still Bullish for Stocks" report
- Global economic briefings, such as a 16-page report on Japan's economy
- The 20-page U.S. Economic Scoreboard publication
- Dozens of U.S. economic indicators each presented in six formats including original text release, charts, tables, and audio
- The Deutsche Bank Alex Brown Weekly Economic Forecast Calendar

BEST OF THE REST

American Demographics

www.demographics.com

Free and Fee-based site

The website for *American Demographics* magazine offers a number of free articles covering numerous aspects of American life. These articles identify trends and place demographic statistics in context. A database of back issues of *American Demographics* contains articles going back to January 1995.

Bureau of Economic Analysis

www.bea.doc.gov

Free site

Many economic analysts recognize the Bureau of Economic Analysis (BEA) as the publisher of the popular "Survey of Current Business," the monthly publication presenting analyses of current U.S. business conditions. The "Survey of Current Business" is available at no charge on the BEA site at *www.bea.doc.gov/bea/pubs.htm.* The BEA site also features statistical data such as gross domestic product tables, selected international statistics, and selected regional data including gross state product and personal income measures.

Bureau of Economic Analysis Regional Economic Measurement Division

www.bea.doc.gov/bea/regional/bearfacts/index.htm

Free site

Economic data, while quite plentiful at the national level, is less bountiful at the regional, state, and local levels. The Federal Reserve District Bank sites discussed above offer regional information, as does the Bureau of Economic Analysis Regional Economic Measurement Division, which produces BEA Regional Facts (BEARFACTS). BEARFACTS consists of computer-generated narratives for states, counties, and metropolitan statistical areas. The narratives describe an area's personal income using current estimates, growth rates, and a breakdown of the sources of personal income.

Business Cycle Indicators

www.tcb-indicators.org

Free and Fee-based site

The Business Cycle Indicators (BCI) database includes data on the economic indicators that have proven to be most useful in determining current conditions and in predicting the future direction of the economy. More than 250 economic data series are in the BCI data set. They cover most major aspects and sectors of the U.S. economy including the composite leading indices, coincident indices, and lagging indices as well as the underlying data series or indicators used to construct these three indices.

Conference Board

www.conference-board.org

Fee-based site

The Conference Board does more than just publish Business Cycle Indicators. The Conference Board is a respected, not-for-profit, nonpartisan organization. More than 3,000 companies and other organizations in 67 countries make up the Conference Board's business membership and research network. This site provides information on the Conference Board's publications, including "International Economic Scoreboard" (covering perspectives and forecasts for 32 major economies) and "Regional Economies and Markets" (a quarterly analysis of trends and prospects in the nine major U.S. regions).

Congressional Budget Office Projections

www.cbo.gov

Free site

Clicking a link on the "Data Highlights" section of the home page of the Congressional Budget Office (CBO) site will take you to the "Current Economic Projections" page. CBO's forecasts for the major macroeconomic variables extend 18 to 24 months in the future. Selected projections are extended out to 10 years.

EconBase

www.elsevier.nl/homepage/sae/econbase

Fee-based site

This site provides access to the EconBase database of economics and finance journals, which includes 19,000 abstracts and 4,500 online papers on a variety of topics. EconBase also produces an econometric time series database that covers subject areas such as economics, business conditions, finance, manufacturing, household income distribution, and demographics. The time series database is available from commercial data providers such as Dialog.

EconData

http://inforumWeb.umd.edu/Econdata.html

Free site

Gratuitous statistics—that's what you will find on EconData site at the University of Maryland. Several hundred thousand economic time series produced by a number U.S. Government agencies are distributed in a variety of formats. The EconData site was developed by Inforum, a research organization at the University of Maryland, with a focus on business forecasting and government policy analysis. Don't confuse this site with Econdata.net at *www.econdata.net*. While the names are similar the sites are not related. Econdata.net does not have any original content but it is an extremely well-organized collection of links to more than 500 economic sites. Econdata.net focuses on gathering links to regional economic data.

Econometrics Laboratory at the University of California, Berkeley

http://elsa.berkeley.edu/eml/emldata.html

Free site

The Econometrics Laboratory is a unit of the Institute of Business and Economic Research in the Department of Economics at the University of California, Berkeley. The laboratory's focus is in the field of computationally intensive econometrics. The site allows access to detailed economic statistics and specialized software tools to assist in the complex analysis. Be aware that access to some databases is restricted to UC students.

Economic Information Systems

www.econ-line.com

Fee-based site

Economic Information Systems is a value-added reseller of economic data. They offer an "Economic Insight Report" that contains charts and analyses for approximately 300 business and economic indicators. State, metro, and county editions of the "Economic Insight Report" are also available. The cost to purchase the state and metro edition runs several thousand dollars for the full series with underlying data, but selected items, including summary versions of the other Insight products, can be downloaded for free.

Economic Policy Institute

http://epinet.org

Free site

The Economic Policy Institute (EPI) is a nonprofit, nonpartisan think tank focusing on the economic condition of low- and middle-income American families. EPI conducts original research and publishes periodicals such as "Paycheck Economics," a collection of articles on wage and income trends, and the "Quarterly Wage and Employment Series," which tracks labor market indicators.

The EPI DataZone (*http://epinet.org/datazone*) presents aggregate time series data that documents historical labor market trends on a state and national basis. Most of the data, which is formatted for downloading into an Excel spreadsheet, is three or more years old.

Economics Research Network

www.ssrn.com/ern/index.html

Free and Fee-based site

The Economic Research Network and its sister organizations, the Financial Economics Network (*www.ssrn.com/fen/index.html*) and the Accounting Research Network (*www.ssrn.com/arn/index.html*) are part of the Social Science Research Network (SSRN). The SSRN is a repository for academic working papers, a number of which were contributed by SSRN Board member Eugene F. Fama. Accessible in the SSRN Electronic Library are abstracts of over 25,900 scholarly working papers and the full text of another 11,700 documents.

Government Information Sharing Project

http://govinfo.kerr.orst.edu

Free site

The Government Information Sharing Project is an Oregon State University project designed to bring together demographic, economic, and educational data. It provides population estimates, regional economic information, and demographics by county. It repackages information found elsewhere on the Internet, but it is nicely organized and easy to navigate.

Haver Analytics

www.haver.com

Fee-based site

Haver Analytics offers detailed economic and financial information to subscribers only. Their primary database of U.S. economic and financial data covers housing, construction, industrial production, interest rates, money supply, federal receipts and outlays, wholesale and retail trade, manufacturers' shipments, inventories and orders, employment, productivity, population, international trade, and business cycle indicators. Haver databases also contain international data, industry information, and regional U.S. data.

Standard & Poor's DRI/McGraw-Hill Research Service

http://dri.standardandpoors.com

Fee-based site

DRI, one of the world's largest economic forecasting firms, produces dozens of databases covering historical and forecast information for domestic and foreign economies. DRI customers can access data on this site through the "Economic Insight" Web-based analysis and forecast program. A selection of free data is also available, including weekly economic analyses and brief discussions of economic conditions in the United States and other industrialized countries.

STAT-USA

www.stat-usa.gov

Fee-based site

Sponsored by the U.S. Department of Commerce, STAT-USA is a fee-based service giving users access to U.S. business, economic, and trade information from the federal government. The site contains current and historical economic and financial data for the domestic economy and international market research, trade opportunities, and country analysis from the National Trade Data Bank.

U.S. Infostore

www.usinfostore.com

Fee-based site

The U.S. Infostore has positioned itself as the low-cost competitor to "big" (its word) economic data services, such as WEFA or Haver Analytics. The primary database at the U.S. Infostore (U.S. Macro Service, which covers 60,000 data series from a variety of mostly governmental data sources) is available on a monthly subscription fee basis. A much smaller database, the Top Business Indicators Service, provides access to more than 150 of the major U.S. macroeconomic time series for free.

WEFA

www.wefa.com

Fee-based site

The WEFA Group evolved from Wharton Econometric Forecasting Associates, which was founded in the 1960s by Nobel laureate Lawrence R. Klein. The volume of data gathering and analysis done by the hundreds of economists employed by WEFA is staggering. WEFA analysts prepare forecasts for 180 countries, conduct specialized client studies, manage databases containing more than 2 million time series, and offer consulting for clients.

The site offers the ability to search their extensive database and view samples of their products, but access to downloadable data is restricted to paying subscribers.

CHAPTER 3

Industry Research

Eva M. Lang

Understanding the dynamics of an industry is valuable to many financial professionals. Business appraisers have no choice but to delve into the industries in which their clients operate. Revenue Ruling 59–60 lays out the factors necessary to consider when performing a business valuation for estate or gift tax purposes. It instructs the appraiser to consider "the economic outlook in general and the condition and outlook of the specific industry in particular."

In order to understand and to locate information on an industry, appraisers need to be able to classify the industry. Until 1997, industries in the United States were classified according to the Standard Industrial Classification (SIC) code system. The SIC classification system provided government-assigned numerical codes for identifying industries, businesses, and products. With the adoption of the North American Free Trade Agreement (NAFTA), the SIC has now been replaced by the North American Industry Classification System (NAICS). The United States, Canada, and Mexico jointly developed NAICS to standardize classification across the three countries. The new classification system allows for the presentation of more detail for the rapidly expanding service sector. Although services now account for the majority of economic activity, they were confined to only a few SIC categories.

Once the industry has been identified, what sort of information are appraisers looking for? What do they want to know about an industry? Below are some questions that should help to define your analysis:

- What is the current state of the industry? Is it a mature industry or still growing?
- What is the structure of the industry? Are there distinct sectors within it?

- Where are the areas of growth? Are new products being introduced?
- How concentrated or dispersed are the companies within the industry? Are there only a few large companies in the industry or lots of small companies?
- What is the competitive environment like? Does price drive competition?
- Who are the consumers in this market? What do you know about them?
- Which companies are market leaders, and how is market share allocated?
- What are the current trends in the industry?
- What is the forecast for industry growth?
- Are there political, economic, or technological factors likely to affect the industry?
- How does technology affect the industry?

Given the number of options for industry data on the Internet, it is necessary to have an understanding of the different types of information that you can expect to find and to have a plan of approach. Trade associations, federal and state governments, brokerage houses, and private research firms all generate industry data. Additionally, there are trade publications as well as industry-specific articles that appear in the general business press.

An effective plan will work from the general to specific and will include a variety of sources. Start with sites that provide information on a variety of industries, such as First Research or the *U.S. Industry & Trade Outlook*. Identify trade associations and see what information they produce. Check for reports from investment analysts available through such sources as Investext and Multex. Search for articles in trade periodicals and the general business press. Check with market research firms about industry reports. The sites listed here will cover all these areas. Because there are hundreds of industries, it is beyond the scope of this chapter to list them all. The chapter focuses on sites that provide access to information on multiple industries and selected major industry sites.

All sites are presented in alphabetical order. The sites listed in the "First and Foremost" section of this chapter are those that the authors have found to be reliable, well organized, and rich sources of information. Sites offering all or part of the data for free are considered more desirable than sites offering similar data for a fee. "Best of the Rest" sites may focus on a niche area, be fee only, or have limited navigation and output features.

FIRST AND FOREMOST

American Society of Association Executives' Gateway

http://info.asaenet.org/gateway/OnlineAssocSlist.html   (Exhibit 3.1)

Free site

It certainly seems that there is a trade association for every activity imaginable, from the American Association of Nude Recreations to the International Parking Institute. It should come as no surprise to learn that there is a trade association for trade association executives. The website of the American Society of Association Executives (ASAE) is an excellent starting place for locating other trade associations. ASAE has complied on its site a "Gateway to Associations," a searchable index of more than 6,500 trade associations. This gateway search page allows you to search for a trade association by name, category, or geographic locations.

If you cannot find the trade association you seek through the ASAE gateway, you can consult other trade association directories on the Internet. They do not tend to be as large as the ASAE gateway, but they may have information on some associations not included in ASAE.

"Associations on the Net" (AON) at *www.ipl.org/ref/AON* is a service of the Internet Public Library that primarily lists nonprofit associations. The AON database contains links to more than 2,000 trade association sites. The associations run the gamut from cultural and art organizations, to political parties and advocacy groups, to labor unions, business organizations, academic societies, and research institutions.

The Marketing Source has assembled a searchable directory of 2,500 trade associations at *www.marketingsource.com/associations*. This site allows you to browse by category as well as search by name or geographic location.

The Associations Database at the Training Forum (*www.trainingforum.com/assoc.html*) includes records for both chambers of commerce and trade associations. While the database is large, with more than 10,000 records, only name, address, and phone numbers are provided. There is no link to the association's website.

There are also a few listings on non-U.S. trade associations, such as the British Trade Association Forum at *www.martex.co.uk/taf/prodfr.htm*, the Directory of South African Associations at *www.icon.co.za/52ireality/brain/associations.html*, the British Directory of Trade Associations at *www.brainstorm.co.uk/TANC/directory/Welcome.html*, and the Industry Canada Industry Associations page at *http://strategis.ic.gc.ca/SSG/mm01428e.html*.

What can you expect to find?

• Searchable index to trade associations on the Internet

asae AMERICAN SOCIETY OF ASSOCIATION EXECUTIVES

Directory services provided by the American Society of Association Executives

Search the Gateway of over 6,589 Associations!

To add your association to ASAE's Gateway to Associations Online, or change your existing information, click the "Yes, add me" button

Yes, add me

Association Name Contains:

Category/Keyword (A-L):
All

Category/Keyword (M-Z):
All

City:
State: All   Country: All

GO!   Clear Form

Please note that the ASAE database is updated frequently, so check it often!

Exhibit 3.1   asae: American Society of Association Executives
Copyright 2000, American Society of Association Executives.

First Research Industry Profiles

www.1stresearch.com   (Exhibit 3.2)

Fee-based site

First Research publishes summary industry analyses on a wide variety of industries. Originally First Research marketed to bankers who needed to understand the industry conditions in which borrowers operated. Over time, other financial professionals in various industries discovered that the reports addressed their needs as well.

The reports focus on understanding industry dynamics relative to suppliers, customers, and competitors. The reports are, on average, about eight pages long and cover industry trends, challenges, and opportunities, and provide links to industry-related sites.

Each report is divided into the following 11 topic headings: Hot Topics, Industry Summary, Industry Overview, Key Questions, Industry Trends & Developments, Industry Threats & Challenges, Industry Opportunities, News & Media Information, Financial Information, Web Site Links, and Glossary of Acronyms.

The reports are updated three to four times a year. The "Hot Topics" section covers any developments in the industry since the last update. The "Industry Summary" defines the industry and touches on key issues. The "Industry Overview" is the meat of the report, a one- to three-page discourse on industry size, markets, competitors, and operating ratios. The "Key Questions" section outlines relevant questions to ask of a company within the industry to assess their ability to compete in the market. The section on "Industry Trends & Developments" identifies changes in the industry, such as the role of consolidation and the level of price competition. The "Industry Threats & Challenges" and "Industry Opportunities" sections outline potential problems and challenges facing those in the industry. "News & Media" covers summaries of recent articles and news stories on the industry. *The Almanac of Business and Industrial Financial Ratios*

FIRSTRESEARCH
ACCURATE INDUSTRY DATA FAST
For Subscription Information Contact First Research at 888-331-2275

industry profiles

◀ BACK TO PROFILES LIST

Industry Profile:	Waste Management
Category:	Services
SIC Codes:	1799, 4212, 4953, 4959
NAICS Codes:	5621, 5622, 5629
Date Last Updated:	July 18, 2000

Link to Profile Chapters:

Hot Topics	Industry Trends & Developments	Financial Information
Industry Summary	Industry Threats & Challenges	Web Site Links
Industry Overview	Industry Opportunities	Glossary of Acronyms
Key Questions	News & Media Information	

Hot Topics

Coming Soon!

Back to Top

Industry Summary

Waste management is a low margin, highly competitive, often unprofitable business, mainly concerned with hauling solid waste and burying it in landfills. It is capital intensive, and evolving technological expertise is now required for many operations. Landfills have higher margins than hauling. Transfer stations now collect local waste for shipment to distant mega-

Exhibit 3.2 FirstResearch: Accurate Industry Data Fast

along with statistics from trade associations and other industry analysts are the sources for the financial information. Each report ends with a list of links to other industry resources and a glossary of terms used in the industry.

The quality of the reports provided is excellent. In charge of industry analysis for First Research is Ingo Winzer, a noted analyst whose views on industry and real estate have been quoted by CNBC, *Barron's, The Wall Street Journal,* and other publications. Winzer, an MIT graduate, has conducted financial investment and strategic corporate research for more than 20 years.

These reports are downloadable from the *www.1stresearch.com* site to subscribers who pay an annual fee. Subscribers can then download an unlimited number of reports, making the cost per report very low for heavy users.

What can you expect to find?

- Detailed downloadable research reports on more than 75 industries

Integra Industry Reports

www.integrainfo.com/products/industrydata/
frprodindata.htm   (Exhibit 3.3)

Fee-based site

Integra collects U.S. government data on private companies and industries primarily from the Internal Revenue Service and the Department of Labor and combines it with proprietary data. From this combined database Integra offers benchmarking data for private companies. It markets three types of industry reports: the "Three-Year Industry Report," the "Five-Year Industry Report," and the "Industry Growth Outlook Report." The three-year and five-year reports contain the following items for each selected industry:

- Historical financial statement data
- Graphs of key operating trends
- Selected financial ratios and industry growth rates

The five-year report has an expanded ratio section and cash flow information. The three-page three-year report is $70 and the nine-page five-year report is $140. The "Industry Growth Report" is a one-page graph of historical and forecasted industry growth compared to the growth of the entire U.S. economy. Integra also sells a five-page "Industry Narrative Report" for $700. That report, a custom report based on the industry sector specified, can be ordered online to be mailed to the customer.

Exhibit 3.3   Integra

Integra offers a free one-page industry benchmarking report at *www. integrainfo.com/free/snapshot/frsnapshot.htm*. After completing a brief registration form, users enter a SIC code and get a one-page report showing industry growth, summary common-size financial statements, and ratios for a single recent year.

What can you expect to find?

• Benchmarking data by industry

International Market Research Mall

www.imrmall.com   (Exhibit 3.4)

Fee-based site

In market research reports, the term "market" can be defined several ways. The market can be an entire industry (e.g., transportation) or it can be an industry subcategory (e.g., short-haul trucking). It may be an industry input (e.g., fuel) or a technology (e.g., global satellite positioning) or a specific product (e.g., tires).

The International Market Research Mall

IMR Sources

- Freedonia
- B.C.C.
- Euromonitor
- Beverage Marketing
- ChemQuest
- C.I.R.
- Find/SVP Reports
- Packaged Facts
- S.B.I.
- Investext/ Markintel

... The Power of Intelligence

Market Research is critical for effective decision making at every level of business planning. The International Market Research (IMR) Mall is the first Web-based community of market research providers. Experienced market research professionals and casual users can search, select, buy, and view full text market research reports online from more than 50 of the world's premier market research publishers. Through the power of The International Market Research Mall you can find and access high-level syndicated market research and retrieve it online within minutes.

browse categories

search titles

search content

Exhibit 3.4 The International Market Research Mall

The International Market Research (IMR) Mall is a collection of reports from a number of market research providers. The reports include both general industry overviews and niche market analyses. The reports cover competitor information, merger and acquisition opportunities, demographics, market forecasts, and trends. The reports include information on both the domestic and foreign market.

At the IMR site users can search, select, buy, and view full-text market research reports online from more than 50 market research publishers. Each record is approximately one page in length and ranges in price from $6 to $40 depending on the publisher. IMR has agreements with some of the most respected market research companies around, including Freedonia, Investext/ MarkIntel, and Faulkner.

The reports are very complete. The following description is from the report titled "Private Companies in the Millwork Industry":

Private companies play a dominant role in the $12.1 billion US millwork market. The industry encompasses over 6,000 companies, the majority of which are small, private, single-establishment firms. However, the industry is fairly concentrated, particularly within the wood window and door segments. Six manufacturers of wood windows, five of which are private, account for nearly 60% of demand, while seven wood door companies, including four private firms, control 33% of demand. This study profiles over 170 privately-held producers and distributors including such industry leaders as Andersen, Jeld-Wen, Marvin Lumber & Cedar, and Pella. The report also presents an overview of the millwork market, including historical data and forecasts for US sales and shipments of wood doors, windows and other millwork by type. Market share, including both public and private companies, is also presented.

The cost for this 120-page report is $3,000.

IMR has set up individual sites for each of its content providers. A list of these sites is available at *http://ecnext.imrmall.com/free-scripts/link2.pl*. If you know that you are only interested in the reports of one provider, say Freedonia or perhaps Beverage Marketing, you can go directly to these subsites and search only for documents from the specific provider.

What can you expect to find?

- Thousands of detailed, but expensive, market research reports
- Market research reports for individual purchase—no subscription necessary

Investext Research Bank

www.investext.com   (Exhibit 3.5)

Fee-based site

Thomson Financial has set up the Research Bank site to provide Web access to three of its databases: Investext Broker Research, MarkIntel Market Research, and Industry Insider Trade Association Research. You may have run across these databases from other vendors as Thomson licenses this content to a host of other sites, including Lexis/Nexis, Dialog, West Law, Northern Light, and Dow Jones Interactive. However, not all the vendors who license the data from Thomson purchase the entire database. The advantage of accessing the data at Research Bank is that you have access to more reports than are available on third-party hosts.

The Investext database contains analysts' reports from the major brokerage houses, such as Morgan Stanley and Merrill Lynch. The analysts' reports cover publicly traded companies and the industries in which they operate. Reports are in Adobe PDF.

MarkIntel market research reports cover industry concerns such as market size, consumer trends, and competition. The reports typically focus on an industry or product and include profiles of key players, market share and demographic trends, forecasts and analyses, and competitive information.

Many of the larger trade associations conduct extensive data gathering and analysis within their industries. Their reports often contain data on industry growth trends, consumer spending habits, sales figures, manufacturing capacity, product developments, market share rankings, and demographics. For some industries that may be smaller or currently out of favor with investment analysts, trade associations may be the only source for data. Often the distribution of this information is limited to the association's members. If the reports are made available to the public, they may be very expensive.

Exhibit 3.5 Thomson Financial

The content on the Research Bank site within the three databases is extensive. The data collection includes more than 2.5 million reports with information on public and private companies and dozens of industry sectors. Information is downloadable by the page, so it is not necessary to purchase the entire report if you only need a portion. Pricing is also by the page, ranging from $6 to $18 depending on the source document. You must have an account before you can search the site. Unfortunately, you cannot set up an account online but must submit an application and wait patiently to be granted access.

What can you expect to find?

- Thousands of analysts' reports from major brokerage houses
- Original research from trade associations—many reports not otherwise accessible to nonmembers
- Market research reports on hundreds of industry groups and subgroups

MarketResearch.com

www.marketresearch.com   (Exhibit 3.6)

Fee-based site

MarketResearch.com is a market research aggregator similar to the International Market Research (IMR) Mall profiled earlier in this chapter. The MarketResearch.com site and the IMR site are really complementary rather than competing sites.

MarketResearch.com has agreements with more than 350 publishers; 50 publishers have agreements to appear on the IMR site. However, the content providers on the IMR site are all market research companies, and all of the data provided is accessible on the site. Many of the content providers on the MarketResearch.com site do not offer electronic access to their products, and most are not market research companies per se. For example, MarketResearch.com lists Gale Research International as a provider of data to the site. But if you use the power search feature of the site to locate the publications provided by Gale Research International, you will find only a listing of books to order by mail.

A number of providers offer products on both sites, but the content available from each publisher varies. For example, at the time of this writing, Freedonia had 581 reports, all electronically accessible, on the IMR site and only 198 on MarketResearch.com site, a number of which were available only by mail. There is no way to search by delivery method, so we were not able to tell what percentage of the content on MarketResearch.com is available electronically.

MarketResearch.com is a good resource for specialty publications and newsletters, such as the *Corporate Growth Report*, a respected weekly newsletter

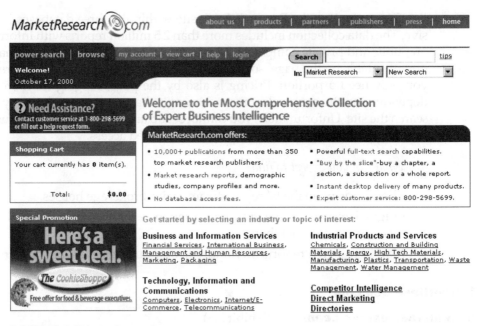

Exhibit 3.6   MarketResearch.com
Copyright © 2000, All Rights Reserved. MarketResearch.com, Inc.

that covers merger and acquisition activity. Content from that report and other newsletters is not available on the MarketResearch.com site, but you can subscribe online.

> *What can you expect to find?*

- Market research reports
- Specialty industry reports

U.S. Industry & Trade Outlook

www.ntis.gov/product/industry-trade.htm   (Exhibit 3.7)

Fee-based site

The *U.S. Industry & Trade Outlook* is a joint project of the International Trade Administration and McGraw-Hill Companies. The *Industry & Trade Outlook* is an excellent compilation of industry-specific data and detailed studies from the government and private sector. It replaces the *U.S. Industrial Outlook,* which the Department of Commerce had published annually until 1994.

Government analysts write most of the material in the *Industry & Trade Outlook* with some assistance from analysts at Standard & Poor's DRI, a division of McGraw-Hill. They primarily rely on federal government reports and statistics from the Census Bureau, including the Census of Manufactures, Census of Minerals, and the Census of Service Industries. Since the federal government data is the most comprehensive and most reliable, the *Industry & Trade Outlook* is a well-respected publication. However, the government is slow in gathering and releasing data, which can cause the analysis in the *Industry & Trade Outlook* to be dated. For example, its 2000 edition was prepared while the 1997 Census data was being released.

Initially the *Industry & Trade Outlook* was available in print and on CD-ROM. Beginning with the 1999 edition, users could download individual chapters from the *Industry & Trade Outlook* in Adobe PDF for a small fee. This is great for users

Exhibit 3.7 U.S. Industry & Trade Outlook

who are interested only in a specific industry sector or special feature. The PDF files contain the full text and all color charts and graphs as they appear in the print edition. All of the introductory and explanatory material included in the front matter of the *Industry & Trade Outlook* is available for free on the site.

What can you expect to find?

- Detailed analyses of the major U.S. industries
- Industry-specific outlooks for international trade
- Illustrative charts and graphs

WEFA

http://nlresearch.northernlight.com/wefa_research.htm   (Exhibit 3.8)

www.multex.com

Fee-based sites

In Chapter 2 we included WEFA as a source of economic data reports. WEFA reports provide in-depth economic and statistical analysis of countries, states, and metropolitan areas as well as industries and commodities. WEFA produces two printed publications, the *Industrial Monitor* and the *Industry Yearbook,* that specifically address industry issues. The *Industrial Monitor* report analyzes trends and the outlook for markets, sales, and pricing in a particular industry. The *Industry Yearbook* report is indexed by SIC code and includes analyses and forecasts of demand conditions, supply conditions, pricing, investment, industry structure, and growth trends.

Individual sections of both publications can be downloaded on a fee-per-view basis from Northern Light and from Multex. Typically, the *Industrial Monitor* reports provided here are detailed reports including both qualitative and statistical analysis of the industry with an assessment of its current health as well as expectations for the future. The "Industrial Monitor Reports" rank the industry in terms of risk and analyzes recent trends. Also included is the outlook for key customer markets, sales, and pricing for a range of important industry segments as well as "changes in the regulatory environment, competitive pressures, and technological change." These reports, which are available on 130 industries, run up to 45 pages long and cost $250 each.

The *Industry Yearbook* offers shorter reports focusing on historical and forecasted demand/supply conditions, price trends, industry structure, and outlook. The *Industry Yearbook* sections are usually four pages or less in length and cost $12.

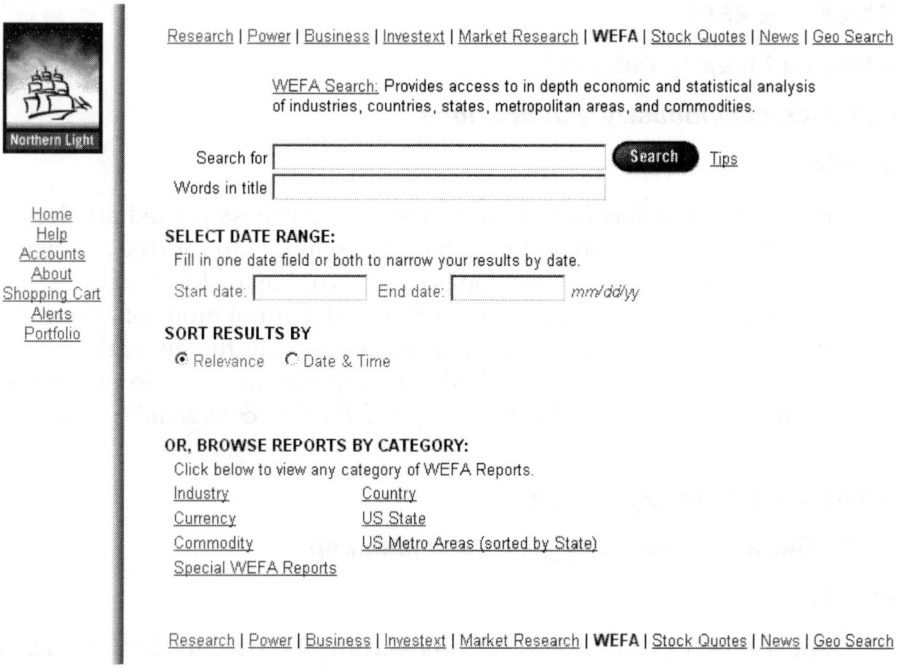

Research | Power | Business | Investext | Market Research | **WEFA** | Stock Quotes | News | Geo Search

WEFA Search: Provides access to in depth economic and statistical analysis of industries, countries, states, metropolitan areas, and commodities.

Northern Light

Home
Help
Accounts
About
Shopping Cart
Alerts
Portfolio

Search for [   ] **Search** Tips
Words in title [   ]

SELECT DATE RANGE:
Fill in one date field or both to narrow your results by date.

Start date: [   ] End date: [   ] *mm/dd/yy*

SORT RESULTS BY
◉ Relevance   ○ Date & Time

OR, BROWSE REPORTS BY CATEGORY:
Click below to view any category of WEFA Reports.
Industry   Country
Currency   US State
Commodity   US Metro Areas (sorted by State)
Special WEFA Reports

Research | Power | Business | Investext | Market Research | **WEFA** | Stock Quotes | News | Geo Search

Exhibit 3.8   Northern Light WEFA Search
Courtesy of Northern Light Technology, Inc.

Both Northern Light and Multex price the reports the same, but finding the reports is easier on Northern Light, which has a special search page for WEFA reports. Here you can search for both WEFA industry reports and the WEFA economic reports mentioned in Chapter 2. On the Northern Light WEFA reports search form, users may search by text or title as well as browse reports by category.

What can you expect to find?

- Detailed industry discussions
- Information on industry structure and outlook
- Industry risk assessment
- Markets and pricing information

BEST OF THE REST

Bpubs.com Industry Publications

www.bpubs.com/Industry_Publications

Free site

Bpubs.com is a specialty search engine for business-related articles. Only articles related to a business topic that can be linked to for free are included. The "Industry Publications" section is categorized by major industry group. Clicking on an industry name takes users to brief annotations of articles with links to the full text. Much of the content comes from the general business magazines, such as the *Economist, Fast Company,* and *Inc.,* and from specialty publications, such as *Network Computing* and *Tourism & Hospitality Journal.*

Business.com Industry Profiles

www.business.com/industry_profiles/index.asp

Free site

The industry profiles on the Business.com site cover the basics, such as size of the industry and major trends. But the major focus of a Business.com profile is how the Internet has affected the industry. Each profile is approximately five pages long and includes graphs and charts. On the profile pages you will find a link to "the Basics," a page that defines the industry, offers background, and puts recent developments in context. Most profiles also contain links to a news page with current news stories and press releases and a time line that outlines the major developments in the industry's history. Because Business.com profiles are written with an eye on the impact of new technology, this is a good place to look for new industries that may not get much coverage from more traditional industry research providers. Check Business.com for profiles of Internet Service Providers (ISPs), the e-commerce industry, and other high-technology industries. The heart of Business.com is not the industry profiles but its directory of hundreds of thousands of business-oriented websites and approximately 10,000 Company Profiles, which contain extensive information about U.S. public company financials, history, press releases, biographies of executives, and time lines of company milestones.

Chicago Mercantile Exchange

www.cme.com

Free site

The Chicago Mercantile Exchange's site is an example of a site that provides information on an industry market segment. It contains information on a variety of futures and options contracts on livestock, dairy, and forest products. You can find not only the current price for pork bellies but also articles such as "A Primer on Pork" and "The Historical Pork Belly Report." These articles provided excellent data on the current market for pork products and the pork production industry. From the home page use the search function to find information on the commodity of your choice.

Frost & Sullivan Research Publications

www.frost.com/rp

Fee-based site

Frost & Sullivan is a well-respected market research firm that produces meticulously detailed, carefully researched, very expensive reports on thousands of industry topics. The MarketResearch.com site mentioned earlier in this chapter provides a selection of Frost & Sullivan reports that can be ordered and mailed to the user. These reports cannot be downloaded. However, on the Frost & Sullivan website, subscribers can download multiple reports electronically for a flat fee. The MarketResearch.com site allows nonsubscribers to purchase reports individually.

Hoover's Industry Snapshots

www.hoovers.com/industry/archive/0,2048,169,00.html

www.hoovers.com/industry/0,1334,18,00.html

Free sites

Hoover's Online, the respected provider of company information, has a collection of 45 industry spotlight profiles tucked away in its archive. The snapshots are well written and packed with graphics, photos, and charts. Each has a glossary of jargon, and there are links from the snapshots directly to financial information on the companies discussed. The current snapshots are located at *www.hoovers.com/industry/0,1334,18,00.html*.

ITA Basic Industries

www.ita.doc.gov/td/bi

Free site

The International Trade Administration (ITA), a part of the U.S. Department of Commerce, runs the Basic Industries program. A broad range of U.S. industries are characterized as Basic Industries, including motor vehicles, automotive parts and accessories, machine tools, chemicals and pharmaceuticals, construction and mining equipment, forest products, metals and materials, energy, and biotechnology. The mission of the Basic Industries program is to enhance international commercial opportunities for these sectors, thereby creating new jobs in the United States.

The ITA Basic Industries website has a collection of "Industry Pages" for each of these basic industry sectors. The "Industry Pages" cover general industry statistics, market research, trade agreements, export data, and trade statistics.

Manufacturing Marketplace

www.manufacturing.net

Free site

The Manufacturing Marketplace site is the self-proclaimed "Online Resource for Manufacturing Solutions." The site has aggregated a great collection of industry-specific articles within manufacturing segments. The site is divided into five communities—Automation & Control, Design, Processes, Plant Operations, and Supply Chain. Use the site's "Search" function to find articles on a particular product or process, such as "steel" or "diecasting." Follow the link "Economics" and you will find a range of current and archived reports on the nation's economy as it relates to manufacturing.

Research at Economy.com

www.economy.com/research

Fee-based site

Economy.com is a member of the Dismal Scientist family of sites mentioned in Chapter 2. On the Economy.com Research page you will find a link to Precis Industry Reports. The reports are four-page analyses and forecasts for 61 major U.S. industries. Each Precis Industry Report covers detailed forecasts for sales, industry drivers, expenses, and profitability, and three pages of industry analysis. Reports are updated three times yearly and are $200 each.

U.S. Census Bureau: Industry Resources

www.census.gov

Free site

> The Census Bureau site is covered in Chapter 2. Here we want to point out that the Census Bureau also collects and disseminates industry information. The "Subjects A to Z" section points you to census publications such as the Census of Construction Industries and the Census of Retail Trade. Most of the files are in Adobe PDF, and can be quite large. Depending on the industry you are researching, the "Current Industrial Reports" can be excellent sources of data.

Valuation Resources Industry Resources Report

http://valuationresources.com/IndustryReport.htm

Free site

> The Valuation Resources site provides a selection of Industry Resources Reports by SIC code. Each Industry Resources Report is a page of links directing the user to other sites with industry information. The report for SIC 5812, Restaurants, includes links to the National Restaurant Association, the *U.S. Industry & Trade Outlook,* and the WEFA *Industrial Monitor.* There are also links to compensation data and to financial benchmarking data. Some links, such as the one to "Financial Studies of the Small Business," take the user to an order form for a publication.

WetFeet.com

www.wetfeet.com

Free site

> Although Wetfeet.com is designed for the job seeker, it provides brief industry overviews of interest to business appraisers. Organized by large industry groupings, the overviews contain background information as well as data on revenues and market share.

CHAPTER 4

Public Company Analysis

Jan Davis Tudor

The market approach to valuing a closely held company requires the appraiser to obtain and analyze a substantial amount of information on publicly traded companies. Even when valuing small companies for which the market approach is not used, due diligence still requires some level of analysis of the public markets.

Where can an appraiser find the public company information necessary to value closely held companies using the market approach? For many years finding and accessing information about public companies was challenging because researchers had to consult a variety of sources, and these sources were often cumbersome, slow, and poorly indexed and archived. But the Internet has changed all of that.

The investment community has embraced the Internet, and virtually every major brokerage firm has a website brimming with investment information. The EDGAR database provides a wealth of financial and competitive information on publicly traded companies. When the EDGAR database was first made available on the Securities and Exchange Commission's (SEC) site, the system was cumbersome to search. Now, private enterprises are providing free and easy access to the database, as well as value-added searching capabilities for a reasonable fee. Internet portals, such as Hoover's, are aggregating company data from a variety of sources and making it available from one website.

While there are hundreds of sources of public company information on the Internet, the sites listed below are those that compile and present information from several sources, add value to the data by presenting sophisticated searching and filtering mechanisms, and are free or reasonably priced.

All sites are presented in alphabetical order. The sites listed in the "First and Foremost" section of this chapter are those that the authors have found to be reliable, well organized, and rich sources of information. Sites offering all or part of the data for free are considered more desirable than sites offering similar data for a fee. "Best of the Rest" sites may focus on a niche area, be fee only, or have limited navigation and output features.

FIRST AND FOREMOST

10Kwizard

www.10kwizard.com   (Exhibit 4.1)

Free site

10Kwizard is a free and popular site for EDGAR filings. It provides not only real-time access to the documents but also the ability to search across the entire EDGAR database by SIC code, phrases, names, form types, date, ticker symbol, partial company name, and keywords. The full-text retrieval tool also allows for the use of the Boolean operators "and," "or," and "not." This advanced search

Exhibit 4.1   10K Wizard Home Page

feature is handy when one wants to find a specific filing for a particular company, or the instances of certain keywords within a filing.

EDGAR filings are available in both RTF and text formats. Researchers can also download filings into common word processor and spreadsheet formats. In addition, users can define and store their own portfolio of searches, and "Alerts," that notify them when a relevant SEC document is filed and available.

What can you expect to find?

- The entire EDGAR database
- Search templates that allow for searching by keyword and SIC code
- Information on insider trading and institutional holdings

CompaniesOnline

www.companiesonline.com

Free site

CompaniesOnline, provided by Lycos and Dun & Bradstreet, contains information on 900,000 public and private companies. The database is searchable by name, Web address, city, state, zip code, area code, Standard Industrial Classification (SIC) code, and ticker. This is a good site for finding basic information about a company and a link to its website.

What can you expect to find?

- For each listing, basic company information from Dun & Bradstreet, such as name, address, map, phone, parent, corporate contact, annual sales, number of employees, trade name(s) industry, link to the company's website, ownership, ticker symbol, and exchange
- A link to Quote.com, which provides a stock quote snapshot, recent headlines, and top analysts' picks

Company Sleuth

www.companysleuth.com

Free site

Once registered with the site, researchers can use this free service to monitor up to 10 public companies. The site also provides a list of the "Top 10 Companies Being Watched" and "Top 10 Stakeouts Requested This Week."

What can you expect to find?

- Notification of new SEC filings, new trademarks and patents, litigation, insider trading, earnings estimates, and analyst reports, discussion group postings, job postings, and press releases
- Reports on the companies e-mailed to users daily

CorporateInformation

www.corporateinformation.com   (Exhibit 4.2)

Free site

CorporateInformation has been providing researchers with a list of comprehensive links to useful websites since 1997 and contains a lot of very useful, free, and unique information. The site's database contains over 350,000 com-

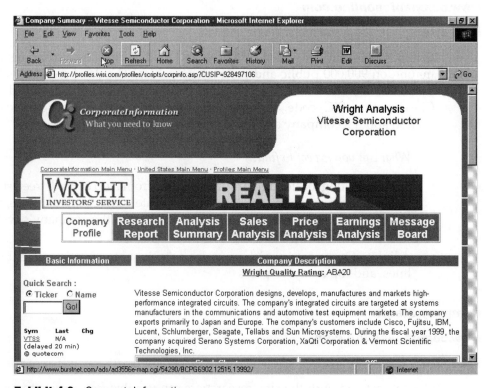

Exhibit 4.2   CorporateInformation

pany profiles and is searchable by company name, ticker, industry, and country. The database also contains over 15,000 research reports.

What can you expect to find?

- The "CI Profile" contains a brief company description, stock chart and recent stock performance, officers, ratio analysis, Wright's rating, and links to historical stock information, SEC filings, news, earnings estimates, patents, and brokerage reports.

- The "Research Report," written by analysts at the Winthrop Corp. and distributed by Wright's Investors' Service, provides a brief analysis of competitors and their recent valuations, sales, profitability, earnings, research and development, inventory, and so on.

- The "Analysis Summary" provides 10 years of stock price, ratios, equity capital, earnings per share and dividends data.

- The "Sales Analysis" provides up to 10 years of sales, sales growth, earnings before interest, taxes, depreciation, and amortization (EBITDA), percentage of sales, income before extra, employees, and sales/employees data.

- The "Price Analysis" provides up to 10 years of quarterly stock price data.

- The "Earnings Analysis" provides up to 10 years of earnings per share and dividends data.

CorpTech

www.corptech.com

Free and Fee-based site

The CorpTech database contains information on approximately 50,000 public and private manufacturers and developers of high-tech products. The companies covered are "primarily emerging small to mid-sized private companies and the operating units of larger corporations." There is no charge to use the site and basic information is free; however, a fee is charged for the more detailed reports. The database is searchable by location and size products, and up to 13 reports can be created.

To access the free data, users can search by company name, stock symbol, product, broad industry category, and person's name. In addition, CorpTech provides "10 Fast Finders"—preformatted searches for common uses of the database. These searches include "Find public companies and operating units," "Find growth companies," "Find competitors," "Find companies by product," and "Find acquisition candidates."

What can you expect to find?

- The free report contains ticker symbol(s), company name, address, telephone, Web address, fax, year business began operations, sales, chief executive officer, and business description.
- Additional free information includes demographics and employment trends, links to high-tech related websites, access to "Company of the Week" and "Industry of the Month."
- The "Standard Profile" ($2–$5) contains sales and employment levels, multiple executive names with their titles and responsibilities, detailed product listings and descriptions.
- The "Extended Profile" ($4–$10) contains the "Standard Profile" as well as up to 10 years' corporate and executive history, up to four years' sales and employee history, rankings, and family reports.
- Links to other resources offering company information.

Edgar Online

www.edgar-online.com   (Exhibit 4.3)

Free and Fee-based site

In addition to free access to EDGAR filings via the company's FreeEdgar service, Edgar Online provides reasonably priced access to EDGAR documents with value-added features. Subscription prices run from $14.25 to $275 a quarter.

What can you expect to find?

- Template-type forms allow for the ability to search across the EDGAR database using a variety of criteria, including company name, ticker, person's name, filing type, industry, location, and date range.
- Each filing has an integrated table of contents. In the HTML version of the document, each section of the filing is outlined so that users can click directly to the section they want to see.
- Import data from any SEC document into Word or WordPerfect format for enhanced formatting including standard pagination. Income Statements, Balance Sheets, and Cash Flow information can be imported into Excel or other spreadsheet programs.
- Links to related company information from other information providers include quotes from PCQuote, charts from BigCharts, business credit reports from Dun & Bradstreet, and other research from Zack's, Wall Street Research Net, Multex, and InsiderTrader.

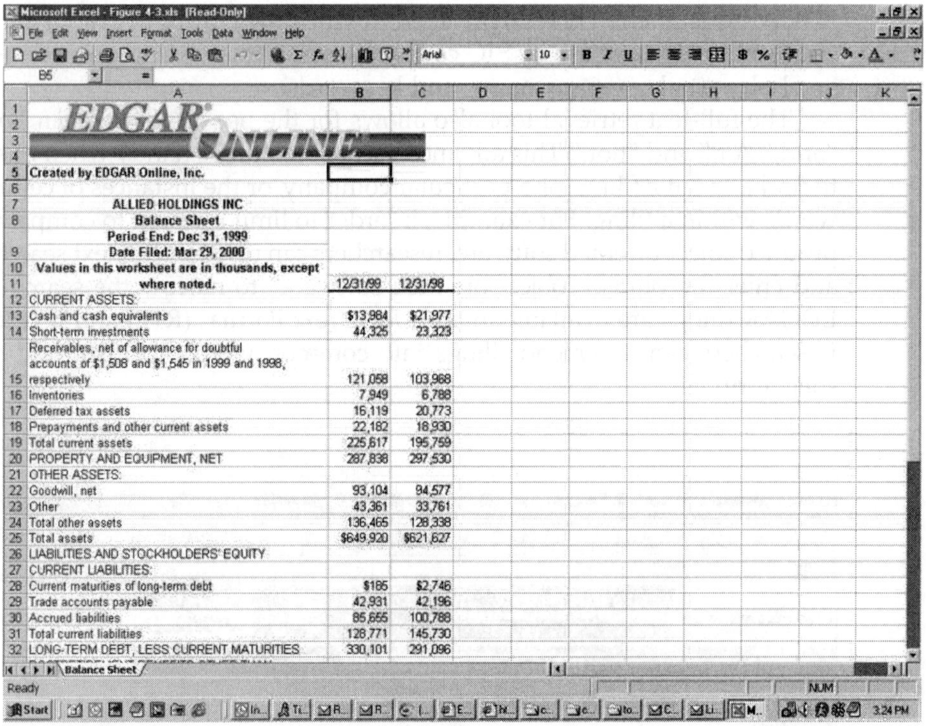

Exhibit 4.3 Allied Holdings, Inc. Balance Sheet
Copyright EDGAR® Online, Inc.® *www.edgar-online.com.*
EDGAR® is a federally registered trademark of the U.S. Securities and Exchange Commission (SEC).
EDGAR Online is not affiliated with or approved by the U.S. Securities and Exchange Commission.
EDGAR Online is a product of EDGAR Online, Inc.

- Users can customize a portfolio of companies, industries, and SEC information to track on a regular basis; order complete printed and bound copies of any EDGAR filing and have them delivered to their office the next day; and set up "WatchLists" to be notified of filings based on user-defined criteria.

FreeEdgar

www.freeedgar.com (Exhibit 4.4)

Free site

FreeEdgar.com is a free and popular source of EDGAR filings. Owned by Edgar Online Inc. (referenced above), the site provides real-time access to

EDGAR documents. FreeEdgar also provides the ability to search across the entire EDGAR database by SIC code, phrases, names, form types, date, ticker symbol, partial company name, and keywords.

The full-text retrieval tool also allows for the use of the Boolean operators "and," "or," and "not." This advanced search feature is handy when one wants to find a specific filing for a particular company, or the instances of certain keywords within a filing. For example, in order to limit a search to companies that produce object-oriented software, researchers can use the "full text search" form and enter the phrase "object oriented software" to narrow the search results. EDGAR filings are available in both Rich Text Format (RTF) and text formats. Researchers can download filings into common word processor and spreadsheet formats.

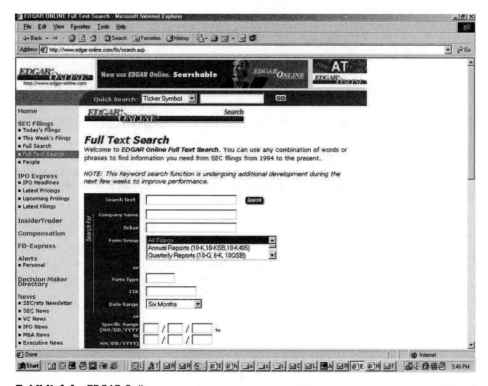

Exhibit 4.4   EDGAR Online

Copyright EDGAR® Online, Inc.® *www.edgar-online.com.*
EDGAR® is a federally registered trademark of the U.S. Securities and Exchange Commission (SEC).
EDGAR Online is not affiliated with or approved by the U.S. Securities and Exchange Commission.
EDGAR Online is a product of EDGAR Online, Inc.

In addition, users can define and store their own portfolio of searches, "WatchLists," which will notify them when a company on the watchlist files with the SEC.

What can you expect to find?

- The entire EDGAR database
- Joint Information's eComp Executive Compensation Database based on the information provided in the proxy statements of publicly traded companies

Hoover's Online

www.hoovers.com   (Exhibit 4.5)

Free and Fee-based site

Approximately 3 million people use Hoover's every month because the site consolidates a lot of useful company information in one easy-to-use place. Hoover's provides content from a variety of vendors, including Powerize, Media General, CBS Marketwatch, Reuters, PR Newswire, and the SEC. While much information is provided for free on the site, personal and corporate memberships allow access to premium company data.

Annual individual memberships are $124.95, and monthly memberships are available. Those interested in corporate memberships need to contact a Hoover's representative.

What can you expect to find?

- Company "capsules" for approximately 14,000 private and public companies. The level of financial data in each capsule depends on whether the company is private or public.
- Each capsule contains a description of the company, its top three competitors, current new stories, financial snapshot, detailed stock quote, links to company press releases, quarterly financials (five quarters), annual financials (three years), list of other companies in the industry, and links to additional fee-based reports on the company by firms such as Dun & Bradstreet, Experian, and Harris Infosource Reports.
- Member benefits include (in addition to the free resources) a more descriptive company "profile," in-depth quarterly (five quarters) and yearly (three years) financials, 10 years of income statement and stock history data, the ability to download the financials into an Excel spreadsheet, and the "Business Boneyard," a database of historical information about

Exhibit 4.5 Hoover's Online
Courtesy of Hoover's Online (www.hoovers.com).

companies that were "swallowed up in mergers and acquisitions, or victims of bad management, market trends, or bankruptcy."

- Paying subscribers can also take advantage of Hoover's "Advanced Search" feature, which allows researchers to search across the database of company capsules by SIC code, financials, number of employees, type of company, and geographic area.

LivEdgar

www.gsionline.com   (Exhibit 4.6)

Fee-based site

Global Securities Information Inc.'s LivEdgar provides reasonably priced access to EDGAR documents. Since such good free access to EDGAR filings exists, one may wonder why someone would pay for the documents. The reason is because LivEdgar has a sophisticated yet easy-to-navigate search interface and a powerful search engine that allows users to search across the entire EDGAR database. EDGAR filings contain an enormous amount of information about a company, and searching the entire database may target data about a private company or licensing agreement.

Users can search by SIC code, phrases, names, form types, date, ticker symbol, partial company name, and keywords as well as with Boolean operators such as "and," "or," "not," "to," and the wildcards "?" and "*". Furthermore, proximity operators such as "W/n" and "P/n" allow researchers to develop very specific concept searches.

Attorneys and their staffs find the "Research Library" provided on the LivEdgar site very helpful because it allows them to target specific types of documents easily. Examples of these preformatted searches include "holding company formation" for corporate structure and "Option Pricing—10 year report" for proxy proposals.

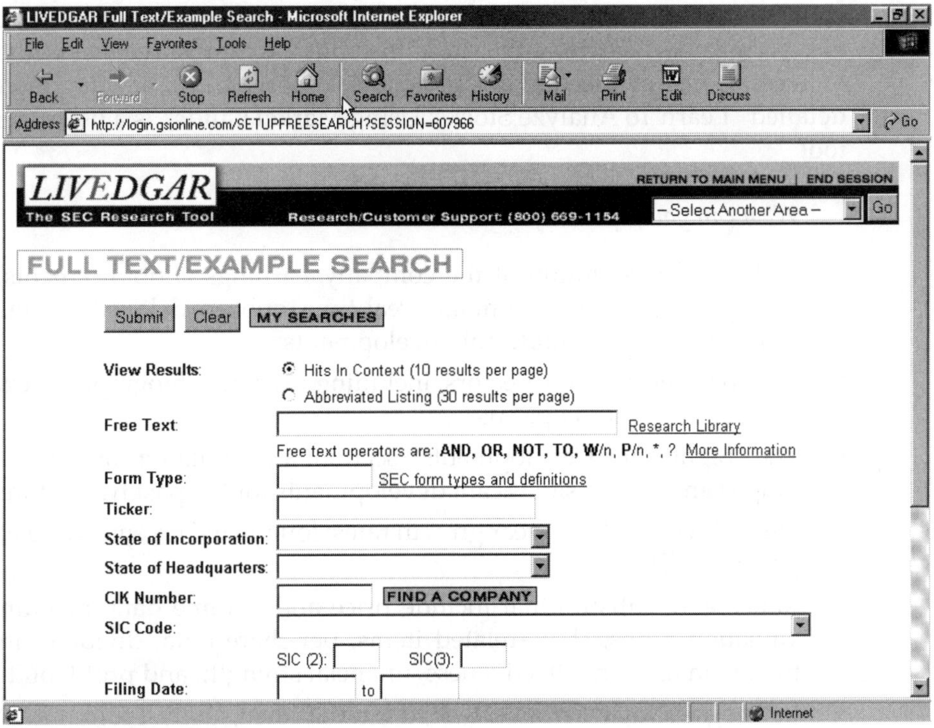

Exhibit 4.6 LivEdgar Full Text/Example Search
Courtesy of Global Securities Information, Inc.

What can you expect to find?

- Template-type search forms and a variety of ways to access EDGAR filings
- Links within each filing that allow users to go directly to the section they want to see without having to wade through the entire document
- Ability to download data into a spreadsheet without any need to format and to download documents into a variety of formats including text, Word, RTF, and Adobe PDF
- Ability to save searches and set up "WatchLists" to be notified of filings based on user-defined criteria

Market Guide

www.marketguide.com

Free and Fee-based site

Market Guide provides detailed company reports for over 10,000 public companies. The amount of information Market Guide provides on public companies is amazing. Searching the site is free, but users must register with the site to access some of the free detailed stock reports and real-time quotes. The detailed "Learn To Analyze Stocks: Using Market Guide" is a useful reference tool.

What can you expect to find?

- A detailed description of the company, earnings announcements, and a "Daily Checkup that contains real-time quotes, delayed quotes, price charts, news, and significant developments
- Data on officers and directors, including executive biographies, executive compensation, and options
- The "Significant Developments" section: a compilation of detailed paragraphs annotating significant developments for the past two to three years
- One-, three-, and five-year growth rates; four years' revenues and earnings per share (EPS)
- Ratios and statistics that include price and volume data including beta, valuation ratios, share-related items, per-share data, dividend information, management effectiveness, financial strength, and profitability
- Earnings estimates from I/B/E/S International, analyst recommendations and revisions, quarterly earnings surprises, historical mean EPS estimate trend, earnings estimates revision summary

- Price performance, institutional ownership, insider trading (previous six months), short interest, price history
- Five years' data from quarterly and yearly income statements, balance sheets, statements of cash flow

Multex Investor

www.multex.com

Free and Fee-based site

The Multex site has "commingled real-time equity research, fixed-income research, morning notes and real-time attributed and consensus estimates." It is a very popular site and has already registered more than 2 million users. The site provides company financial data from Market Guide and a search feature that allows researchers to search for documents by ticker symbol, company name, industry, brokerage firm, analyst, geographic region, country, currency, and/or full-text words and phrases, as well as company name, broad industry groupings, analyst, or research provider, such as Adams, Harkness & Hill. Two types of reports are available: free reports and pay-per-view reports. The price of each report is listed next to the headlines; reports range from $5 to $150.

What can you expect to find?

- A database of more than 300,000 full-text broker research reports from over 250 providers in Adobe PDF format, including all original text, charts, graphs, tables, color, and document formatting
- Real-time attributed and consensus earnings estimates
- Financial and business information from more than 700 of the world's leading brokerage firms, investment banks, and independent content providers

Northern Light

www.northernlight.com

Free and Fee-based site

Northern Light is both an Internet search engine and a collection of materials licensed from database providers such as Thomson Financial. Users can search the system and use material retrieved from the Internet for free; articles and analysts' reports incur a charge.

The authors recommend this database for research on public companies because it provides easy and cost-effective access to quality material that is otherwise difficult to find.

What can you expect to find?

- Two weeks of current news from a variety of newspapers for free
- Reports from the Investext database (see more descriptive information in Chapter 3) sold by the page—a cost-effective way of finding analysis and forecasts for publicly traded companies
- Journal articles from thousands of trade publications

The Wall Street Journal Briefing Books

www.wsj.com

Fee-based site

Subscribers to the online version of *The Wall Street Journal* have free access to the "Briefing Books"—reports that contain background and financial information on publicly traded companies. In addition, subscribers have access to the entire Dow Jones Publication Library, which contains current and archived articles from thousands of trade journals and newspapers from around the world.

The Business Briefings are nicely formatted and easy to read. Subscriptions for the online version are $59 a year or $29 a year if one subscribes to the print version. Articles from the Dow Jones Publications Library run $2.95 each.

What can you expect to find?

- A financial overview in both chart and text format
- Stock charts and earnings estimates
- News releases from Dow Jones Newswire
- Links to related news from leading business publications and the *Journal*, press releases, and stock quote details

The Wall Street Research Network

www.wsrn.com

Free and Fee-based site

The Wall Street Research Network (WSRN) is a popular site despite its cluttered appearance. Like most financial sites, WSRN compiles a wealth of company information, much of which is free. The monthly fee for premium data is $9.95; discounts are given for six-month and yearly subscriptions.

What can you expect to find?

- The free information includes detailed quotes, charts, news, company description, "Tear Sheet Fundamentals" with seven years' income statement, balance sheet, ratios, EPS estimates, and company-to-industry ratios.

- Fee-based data includes shares outstanding, shares outstanding chart, annual and quarterly EPS history, historical quotes, dividends and splits history, and the "Advanced Searching" feature.

- One-time research needs, such as a download of 10 years of stock prices, are available for $2.50 to $5.

- WSRN/BASELINE company profiles are available for $1.99 each.

BEST OF THE REST

144A/Private Placement Database

www.gsionline.com

Fee-based site

Global Securities Information Inc. (GSI) offers a database of 144a and Regulation S offering circulars. GSI has negotiated with broker-dealers from over 80 countries to secure these documents. The database contains documents from April 1990 to the present.

Dot Com Layoff Tracker

http://search.thestandard.com/texis/trackers/layoff

Free site

Each quarter TheStandard.com publishes and charts layoffs within the dot.com world. The chart contains the name of each company and the industry in which it participates, date of layoffs, the number of people laid off, and explanation.

ELibrary

wwws.elibrary.com

Fee-based site

For $9.95 a month researchers can access journal and news articles, books, and television and radio transcripts. Many of the sources included in ELibrary are trade association magazines and newspapers from smaller cities. These types of publications often run stories on local or specialized businesses and can provide more detailed information than might be found elsewhere.

Ex-Exec Tracker

http://search.thestandard.com/texis/trackers/exec

Free site

Each quarter TheStandard.com also publishes and charts "a rundown of who's leaving what company and why (according, at least, to the company's press release)." The chart contains the names of the ex-executives, the date of departure, the to and from companies, their explanation, time served, and stock market reaction (if the company was public).

Goldman Sachs Research on Demand

www.gsnews.com

Free and Fee-based site

Once registered with the site, researchers can access Goldman Sachs investment reports. Abstracts are free; however, retrieving entire reports requires a subscription.

IPO Express

www.edgar-online.com/ipoexpress

Free site

IPO Express is a database of over 2,500 IPO filings and over 1,500 underwriters, and is a good place to look for the latest IPO pricings and filings, upcoming filings, postponements, withdrawals, international IPOs, and IPOs by industry, underwriter, and state.

Merrill Lynch Online

http://askmerrill.com/mlol/main/index.asp

Fee-based site

Once registered with the site, researchers can obtain a 30-day trial of Merrill Lynch's investment analyst reports online.

The Public Register

www.publicregister.com   (Exhibit 4.7)

Free site

The Public Register provides free copies of annual reports for 2,300 public companies. Researchers must order them and they are delivered via regular mail.

In addition to providing an order form for the annual report, The Public Register provides links to the company's home pages, Zack's Research Reports, Wall Street Snapshots, and the Silicon Investor Form.

SEDAR (System for Electronic Document Analysis and Retrieval)

www.sedar.com

Free site

SEDAR, the System for Electronic Document Analysis and Retrieval, is the electronic filing system for public companies and mutual funds in Canada.

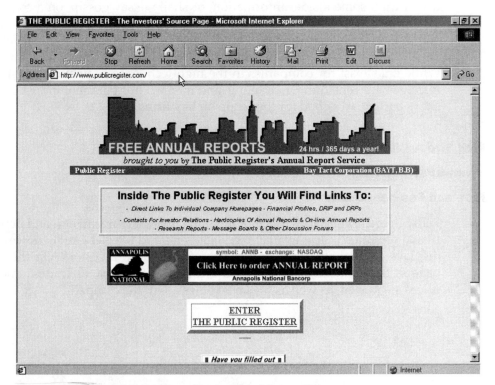

Exhibit 4.7 The Public Register—The Investors' Source Page

The SEDAR website contains copies of the disclosure documents filed in the system as well as profiles containing basic information about each company or mutual fund group.

Silicon Investor

www.siliconinvestor.com

Free site

Researchers interested in tech companies will benefit from the current financial information published on the site as well as the discussions about particular stocks.

Vault Reports

www.vaultreports.com

Free site

If you want some insider information, or shall we say gossip, on a company, check The Vault. This site is geared toward those looking for a job. The level and amount of information provided depends on how much the folks at The Vault could compile from surveys, inside contacts, and "message boards." While links exist for companies in the high-tech, energy, finance, healthcare, management consulting, marketing, and media/entertainment industries, the site is particularly good for the scoop on law firms.

Wall Street City

www.wallstreetcity.com   (Exhibit 4.8)

Free and Fee-based site

Wall Street City provides much of the same financial information and descriptive information that is available on Hoover's and Market Guide; however, it displays additional graphs and charts of interest to investors. On the same page as the financial snapshot for a company, "The Last 10 Trades" and the prices are posted, as well as the latest news about the company.

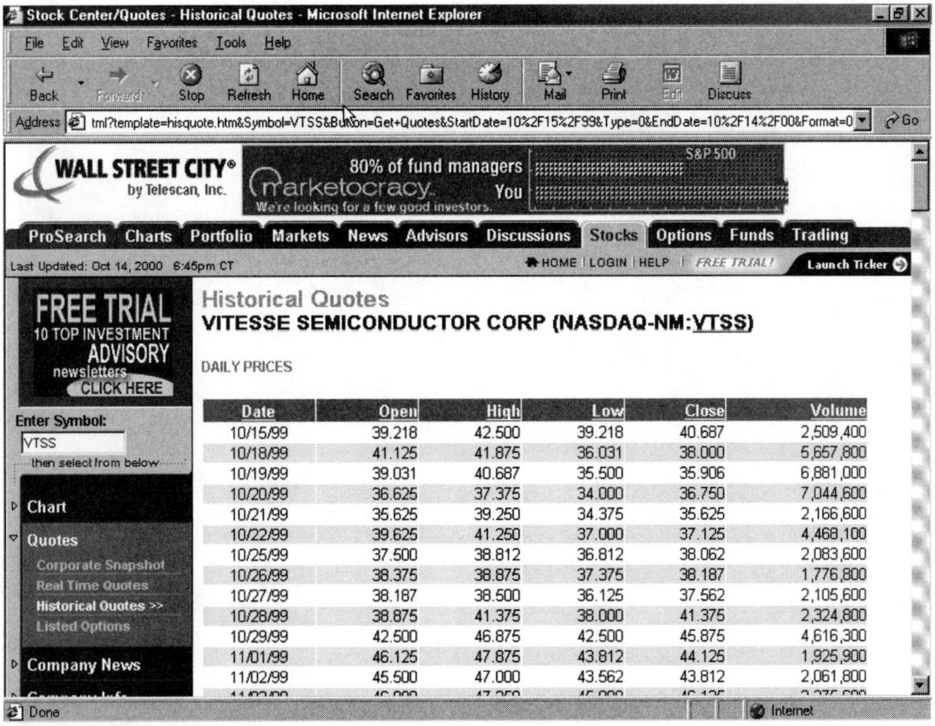

Date	Open	High	Low	Close	Volume
10/15/99	39.218	42.500	39.218	40.687	2,509,400
10/18/99	41.125	41.875	36.031	38.000	5,657,800
10/19/99	39.031	40.687	35.500	35.906	6,881,000
10/20/99	36.625	37.375	34.000	36.750	7,044,600
10/21/99	35.625	39.250	34.375	35.625	2,166,600
10/22/99	39.625	41.250	37.000	37.125	4,468,100
10/25/99	37.500	38.812	36.812	38.062	2,083,600
10/26/99	38.375	38.875	37.375	38.187	1,776,800
10/27/99	38.187	38.500	36.125	37.562	2,105,600
10/28/99	38.875	41.375	38.000	41.375	2,324,800
10/29/99	42.500	46.875	42.500	45.875	4,616,300
11/01/99	46.125	47.875	43.812	44.125	1,925,900
11/02/99	45.500	47.000	43.562	43.812	2,061,800

Exhibit 4.8 Wall Street City
Provided by Telescan, Inc. 800-324-4692.

CHAPTER 5

Private Company Analysis

Jan Davis Tudor

While numerous Internet sites that are chock-full of detailed information on public companies are available, the same cannot be said for private companies. Because private companies are not subject to the same reporting requirements as public companies, detailed financial information on privately held businesses is simply not available.

However, the Internet has facilitated the process of gathering information on private companies for the purposes of competitive intelligence. Company websites typically provide information about the firm's products, mission statement, personnel, and locations, and sophisticated Internet directories can lead researchers to these sites. Newspapers and magazine articles that typically carry stories about private companies are now available on the Net for free or a small charge. Credit reporting agencies now make their databases available to the public, and researchers can screen those databases to get basic financial information, create marketing lists, and research the competition.

All sites are presented in alphabetical order. The sites listed in the "First and Foremost" section of this chapter are those that the authors have found to be reliable, well organized, and rich sources of information. Sites offering all or part of the data for free are considered more desirable than sites offering similar data for a fee. "Best of the Rest" sites may focus on a niche area, be fee only, or have limited navigation and output features.

FIRST AND FOREMOST

Business Filings Databases

www.llrx.com/columns/roundup4.htm

Free and Fee-based site

Seventy-five percent of states in the United States require that some level of business and corporate filings be made available online. Attorney and author Kathy Biehl developed this site to share with researchers what each state has made available on the Web in terms of corporate and business filings.

What can you expect to find?

- Organized by state, links to database of publicly available business and corporate filings
- "If a state is not on the list, it has not posted corporate records online."

CompaniesOnline

www.companiesonline.com

Free site

CompaniesOnline, provided by Lycos and Dun & Bradstreet, contains information on 900,000 public and private companies. The database is searchable by name, Web address, city, state, zip code, area code, SIC code, and ticker. This is a good site for finding basic information about a company and a link to its website.

What can you expect to find?

- For each listing, basic company information from Dun & Bradstreet, such as name, address, map, phone, parent, corporate contact, annual sales, number of employees, trade name(s) industry, link to the company's website, ownership, ticker symbol, and exchange

CorporateInformation

www.corporateinformation.com   (Exhibit 5.1)

Free site

CorporateInformation has been providing researchers with a list of comprehensive links to useful business-related websites since 1997. The site's database contains over 350,000 company profiles. After typing in the name of a company, researchers will receive a list of links to related sites about that company. CorporateInformation claims that it links only to sites that contain worthwhile information.

When searching by company name, researchers should enter as many words from the company's name as possible in order to retrieve a relevant list of sites. If the company has two words in its name, type the two words in quotes.

What can you expect to find?

- Links to websites that contain information about the subject company, for example, the search "Kohler Co." retrieved links to a Hoover's capsule, the *Forbes* "Private 500" list, and the Telecommunications Industry Association's "Buyer's Guide"

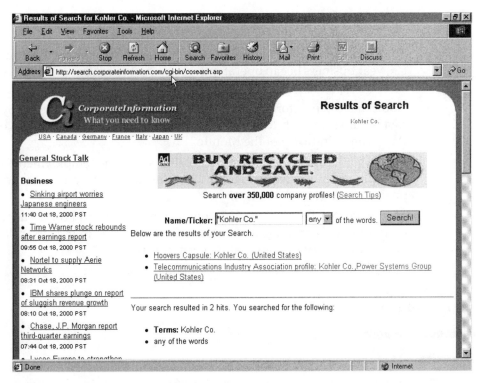

Exhibit 5.1 Results of Search for Kohler Co.

CorpTech

www.corptech.com

Free and Fee-based site

The CorpTech database contains information on approximately 50,000 public and private manufacturers and developers of high-tech products. The companies covered are "primarily emerging small to mid-sized private companies and the operating units of larger corporations." There is no charge to use the site and basic information is free; however, a fee is charged for more detailed reports. The database is searchable by location and size products, and up to 13 reports can be created.

To access the free data, users can search by company name, stock symbol, product, broad industry category, and person's name. In addition, CorpTech provides "10 Fast Finders"—preformatted searches for common uses of the database. These searches include "Find public companies and operating units," "Find growth companies," "Find competitors," "Find companies by product," and "Find acquisition candidates."

What can you expect to find?

- The free report contains company name, address, telephone, Web address, fax, year business began operations, sales, chief executive officer, and business description.
- Additional free information includes demographics and employment trends, links to high-tech related websites, access to "Company of the Week" and "Industry of the Month."
- The "Standard Profile" ($2–$5) contains sales and employment levels, multiple executive names with their titles and responsibilities, detailed product listings, and descriptions.
- The "Extended Profile" ($4–$10) contains the "Standard Profile" as well as up to 10 years' corporate and executive history, up to four years' sales and employee history, rankings, and family reports.
- Links to other resources offering company information.

dot com directory

www.dotcom.com

Free site

The dot com directory is a useful tool for finding not only a company's presence on the Internet but also where the company is located and how to get there. With the dot com directory, users also can look up ownership information by website address.

What can you expect to find?

- The business's name, address, telephone, website, and industry
- The ability to purchase a business credit report or find subsidiaries or divisions
- More extensive information on public companies, including ticker symbols, company-owned websites, news, executives, competitors, select financials, and more

Dun & Bradstreet

www.dnb.com/dnbhome.htm   (Exhibit 5.2)

Fee-based site

Dun & Bradstreet is well known for its credit data, which is used for marketing, prospecting, purchasing, and receivables management purposes. At the company's website researchers can search the database of more than 26 million companies. Financial data is available for "some" larger private companies and is provided in the "Business Information Reports" and the "Comprehensive Report."

D&B obtains its data from company contacts, trade tapes, courthouses, government sources, banks, customers, trade associations, business-to-business publications, and financial institutions. D&B updates the information through interviews, direct mail programs, updates of reported bankruptcies, suits, liens, judgments, UCC filings and payment experiences, and investigations prompted by customers' inquiries.

What can you expect to find?

- The D&B "Business Information Report," which includes company summary and analysis, history, public filings, payment summary, and finance and operation; cost: $89
- "Business Background Reports," which do not have credit data but contain information provided to D&B by the subject company itself; cost: $23
- The D&B "Comprehensive Reports," which allows researchers to compare key business ratios against industry norms, and obtain a brief summary report including background information on the company and its senior management; cost: $105

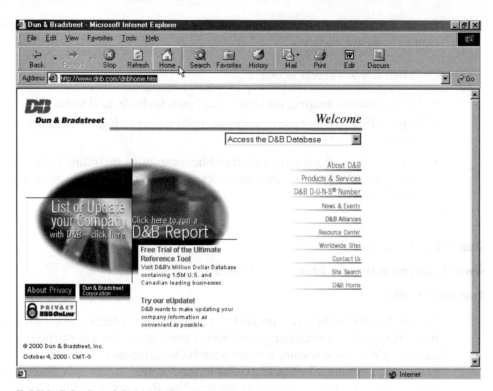

Exhibit 5.2   Dun & Bradstreet
The Dun & Bradstreet Corporation, 2000.

- The D&B "Supplier Evaluation Report"; cost: $93
- The D&B "Credit Scoring Report"; cost: $49

Experian

www.experian.com/catalog_us/index.html

Fee-based site

The Experian (formerly TRW) database contains over 13 million U.S. companies and is used by people who want credit information on a business. While searching the database is free, researchers must first register with this site. Unfortunately, to find information about a particular company, users must enter the company name with its complete address. When comprehensive information is available, Experian provides a full Snapshot report, including a credit risk category, for $14.95. When little information is available, a limited report without the risk category costs $5.

What can you expect to find?

- The Snapshot report contains company name and address, legal filings, payment and trend behavior, and company and financial services history.
- The Business Public Records search contains Uniform Commercial Code data, bankruptcy and tax lien information, as well as additional corporate records.

Forbes Magazine and the Forbes Private 500

www.forbes.com

Free site

Forbes has reported on private companies for many years. Each year *Forbes* publishes "The Private 500," an annual directory of the 500 largest privately held U.S. corporations, "taking into consideration revenues and number of employees." In addition, each year *Forbes* publishes the "Forbes Best Small Companies," many of which are private.

What can you expect to find?

- Extensive database of small companies dating back to 1996
- Current and earlier editions of the "The Private 500"
- Complete free archive of *Forbes* articles from the 1997 to the present

Hoover's Online

www.hoovers.com   (Exhibit 5.3)

Free and Fee-based site

While Hoover's is known for its in-depth profiles of public companies, the site also provides quite a bit of information on selected private companies.

What can you expect to find?

- Company "capsules" on private companies containing varying degrees of financial information
- "Key people" in the company
- Competitors
- News and trade publication articles on the company as well as press releases

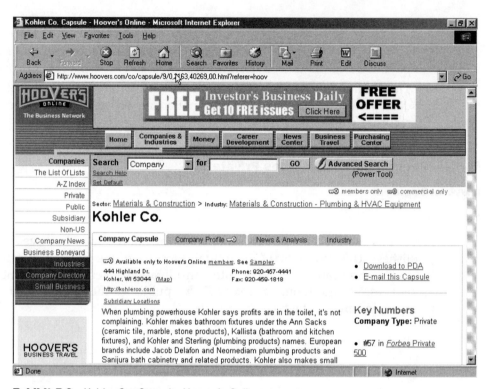

Exhibit 5.3   Kohler Co. Capsule–Hoover's Online
Courtesy of Hoover's Online (www.hoovers.com).

Inc. Magazine and the Inc. 500

www.inc.com

Free site

Inc. magazine has always featured stories on private companies as well as the yearly Inc. 500, an "Annual List of America's Fastest-Growing Private Companies."

What can you expect to find?

*   A free archive of articles dating back to the early 1990s to the present
*   The current Inc. 500 and related articles as well as a searchable database of the companies included in the Inc. 500 since 1982

Northern Light

www.northernlight.com

Free and Fee-based site

As described elsewhere, Northern Light is both an Internet search engine and a collection of magazine, journal, and news articles. Publications often run stories on local or specialized businesses and can provide more detailed information than might be found elsewhere. The authors recommend Northern Light for research on private companies because the site provides a powerful and sophisticated Internet and search engine as well as easy and cost-effective access to quality material that is otherwise difficult to find.

What can you expect to find?

- Two weeks of current news from a variety of newspapers for free
- Thousands of articles from popular and obscure magazines and journals for $2.95

TechSavvy

www.techsavvy.com

Free site

TechSavvy.com "provides a broad base of technical, engineering, design, maintenance and procurement information." The site consists of a database of databases from Information Handling Services Inc., which includes "Commercial/Industry Standards" from Global Engineering Documents, "US Military Documents," "Company Directory," "Historical Data," and "Parts Information."

What can you expect to find?

- An index of in-depth company profiles, "business centers" with links to company websites, "business cards" from Harris InfoSource, names of decision makers, and product descriptions, for over 5,500 product categories

Thomas Register of American Manufacturers

www3.thomasregister.com/index.cgi

Free site

The *Thomas Register of American Manufacturers* is a well-known and established index of manufacturers. It is a great source for finding U.S. and Canadian companies and what each company does; users also can find out which companies make a certain type of product. The database of 155,000 is searchable by company name, product or service, and brand name.

What can you expect to find?

- Basic business information such as name and address
- Links to company catalogs and websites for many companies in the database

BEST OF THE REST

A.M. Best Insurance Company Directory and Reports

www3.ambest.com/ratings/Advanced.asp

Free and Fee-based site

An extensive database of nearly 6,000 life/health, property/casualty, and international insurance companies are provided on the A.M. Best "Ratings and Analysis" website. Profiles include company name, address, phone, domicile, affiliation or membership, A.M. Best and NAIC numbers, Web address, ticker symbol, date business commenced, and rating. Researchers may purchase complete company reports.

Business CreditUSA.com

www.businesscreditusa.com/index.asp

Free site

Business CreditUSA.com is an "Internet business credit portal" that provides free business credit reports for public and private U.S. companies and executives. The database currently has 12 million records. According to the company, approximately 55 percent of the records are from businesses with less than four employees. This is a good source for finding fax, telephone, and address data, verifying a business's existence and stability, and generating sales leads.

The database is searchable by company or executive name, city, state, telephone number, or American Business Information (ABI) number. Each report contains the company name, address, names of select executives, phone, fax, credit rating, number of employees, ticker symbol, SIC code(s), competitors, and news headlines.

Dot Com Layoff Tracker

http://search.thestandard.com/texis/trackers/layoff

Free site

Each quarter TheStandard.com publishes and charts layoffs within the dot.com world. The chart contains the name of each company and the industry in which it participates, date of layoffs, the number of people laid off, and explanation.

EDGAR

www.10Kwizard.com   (Exhibit 5.4)

www.edgar-online.com

www.freeedgar.com

www.gsionline.com

Free and Fee-based sites

The EDGAR database was discussed in detail in Chapter 4. While the database is comprised of detailed information filed by public companies, users may find information on a particular private company. In certain instances, a public company may have referenced a private company because of an acquisition or licensing agreement.

Because the providers of the EDGAR database have developed search interfaces that allow researchers to search by keyword, a quick search on a private company's name may yield some information.

ELibrary

wwws.elibrary.com

Fee-based site

For $9.95 a month researchers can access journal and news articles, books, and television and radio transcripts. Many of the sources included in ELibrary are trade association magazines and newspapers from smaller cities. These types of publications often run stories on local or specialized businesses and can provide more detailed information than might be found in the more general business publications.

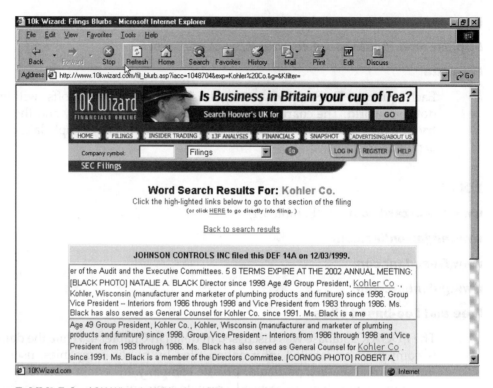

Exhibit 5.4   10K Wizard: Kohler Inc. filings

Ex-Exec Tracker

http://search.thestandard.com/texis/trackers/exec

Free site

Each quarter TheStandard.com publishes and charts "a rundown of who's leaving what company and why (according, at least, to the company's press release)." The chart contains the names of the ex-executives, the date of departure, the to and from companies, their explanation, time served, and stock market reaction (if the company was public).

Franchise 500

www.entrepreneur.com

Free site

Entrepreneur magazine offers a database containing information on franchises and their rankings, business descriptions, links to their websites, an annual breakdown of the number of units owned since 1997, financial information, and additional contact information.

Vault Reports

www.vaultreports.com

Free site

If you want some insider information, or shall we say gossip, on a company, check The Vault. This site is geared toward those looking for a job. The level and amount of information provided depends on how much the folks at The Vault could find from surveys, inside contacts, and "message boards." While links exist for companies in the high-tech, energy, finance, healthcare, management consulting, marketing, and media/entertainment industries, the site is particularly good for the scoop on law firms.

CHAPTER 6

Salary, Executive Compensation, and Surveys

Jan Davis Tudor

Salary and executive compensation and surveys are sought after for a number of reasons. In some cases, boards of directors often need to justify their CEO pay allocations to shareholders, executives wish to assess the adequacy of a proposed compensation plan, or job seekers want to know the going salary in their occupation. The Internet has become a very useful tool to help researchers get their hands on the surveys, because it allows trade associations, database providers, consulting firms, and dot.coms a forum in which to make their surveys available for free or for a fee.

The Internet sites listed in this chapter include both "executive compensation" surveys, which typically include the compensation packages of a company's executives and top managers, and "salary surveys," which typically include the salaries of all workers within an industry, from entry level to the executive.

It is important to remember that these surveys provide not only annual salary data but also details about the executive bonuses, stock options, long-term incentive plans, and other noncash compensation. So while many sites provide survey excerpts, it may be necessary to pay for the entire report to get the whole picture of the compensation package. In any case, the Internet has made it much easier to find salary and executive compensation surveys.

All sites are presented in alphabetical order. The sites listed in the "First and Foremost" section of this chapter are those that the authors have found to be reliable, well organized, and rich sources of information. Sites offering all or part of the data for free are considered more desirable than sites offering similar data for a fee. "Best of the Rest" sites may focus on a niche area, be fee only, or have limited navigation and output features.

FIRST AND FOREMOST

Abbott, Langer & Associates, Inc.

www.abbott-langer.com   (Exhibit 6.1)

Free and Fee-based site

This consulting firm has been performing compensation surveys since 1967 and provides quite a bit of the data from their published surveys for free on their website. The site is organized by 12 subjects and a "What's New" section.

What can you expect to find?

- The "free summary data" link provides four to five summary paragraphs and a chart of median annual incomes for a range of positions, including president and chief financial officer.

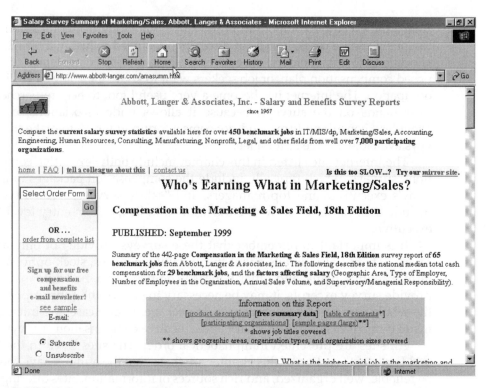

Exhibit 6.1   Salary Survey Summary of Marketing/Sales, Abbott, Langer & Associates, Inc.

- The complete reports sell for an average of $500 and can be ordered on-line.

America's Career InfoNet

www.acinet.org/acinet   (Exhibit 6.2)

Free site

America's Career InfoNet (ACINet) is sponsored by the DOL and allows Internet searchers to access America's Labor Market Information System (ALMIS). The database consists of information pulled from a variety of state and federal government agencies, such as the U.S. Bureau of Labor Statistics (BLS) and various state Departments of Labor.

Researchers can access salary and wage data either by a keyword or menu search. The menu search contains a list of 22 general "job families" derived from the BLS Occupational Employment Statistics (OES) occupation list. Within each "job family" exists a more detailed list of occupational titles. Determining which category contains the job title needed sometimes is difficult;

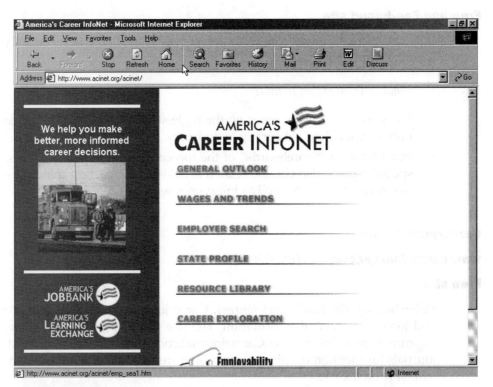

Exhibit 6.2   America's Career InfoNet

using the keyword search feature may be more straightforward. The search can then be defined by geographic area, such as state, district, or territory.

What can you expect to find?

- An array of occupational, demographic, and labor market information at the local, state, and national levels
- The ability to compare the average salary for one profession with that of another
- The ability to determine the average number of people hired for a particular profession within a specific area
- Continually updated links to career profiles in other publications, such as the Princeton Review and the Occupational Outlook Handbook, and local, state, and national career and labor market information sites

Business Week

www.businessweek.com

Free and Fee-based site

Business Week's annual compensation survey is available in its entirety from the magazine's website.

What can you expect to find?

- The surveys typically focus on the highest paid executives in the country rather than a detailed survey by industry.
- In addition to "Scoreboards" of the top-compensated professionals, these special reports also contain related articles on the current trends in executive compensation as well as interviews with CEOs.

Careerjournal.com

www.careerjournal.com   (Exhibit 6.3)

Free site

Published by *The Wall Street Journal*, Careerjournal.com is a portal of salary and job search–related information. The site provides wage and salary data organized by industry. The Careerjournal.com staff screens news and trade journals for mention of salary surveys and trends. The articles are then made available on the site.

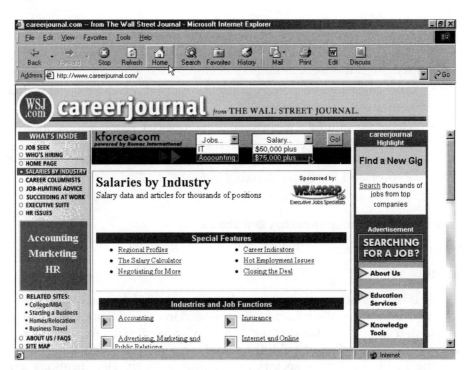

Exhibit 6.3 careerjournal.com—from *The Wall Street Journal*

What can you expect to find?

- Articles and salary tables for each industry sector
- A section called "Regional Profiles" that contains news items that focus on labor issues in different regions of the country; many of the news stories are from the *The Wall Street Journal*

eComp Corporate Database

www.ecomponline.com

Fee-based site

In addition to eComp's free database mentioned earlier in this chapter, Joint Information Inc. provides eComp Corporate Database. This database, available on an annual subscription basis, allows for sophisticated searching across a database of over 48,000 executives employed by public companies and the ability to create unique peer groups based on multiple criteria.

What can you expect to find?

- The ability to build a peer group of companies based on state, sector, industry, revenue, assets, or number of employees
- The ability to save, edit, and delete your peer groups, as well as download into spreadsheet format
- Generate multiple reports such as Direct Compensation Report, Total Compensation Report, Long Term Compensation Report, Fiscal Year End Options Report, Exercised/Realized Option Report, Unexercisable Option Report, and Executive Ranking Report

eComp Executive Compensation Database

www.ecomponline.com   (Exhibit 6.4)

Free site

This new database allows researchers to make quick executive compensation reports based on the information provided in the proxy statements of publicly traded companies. Researchers can search an entire database of the executive compensation data of public companies by company name, ticker, or one of the 12 Market Guide sectors or 100-plus industry classifications and view compensation data without having to wade through the entire SEC filing. Joint Information has plans to make the database searchable by SIC and NAICS codes.

What can you expect to find?

- Executive compensation information on over 48,000 executives employed by public companies (This database eliminates the need to dig through SEC filings for compensation data)
- Documents for the information you need
- The ability to search by state, sector, industry, company name, or ticker symbol
- The ability to create a Summary Compensation Report, Fiscal Year End Option Report, and Unexercised Option Report for one company at a time
- The ability for view multiple reports for each company

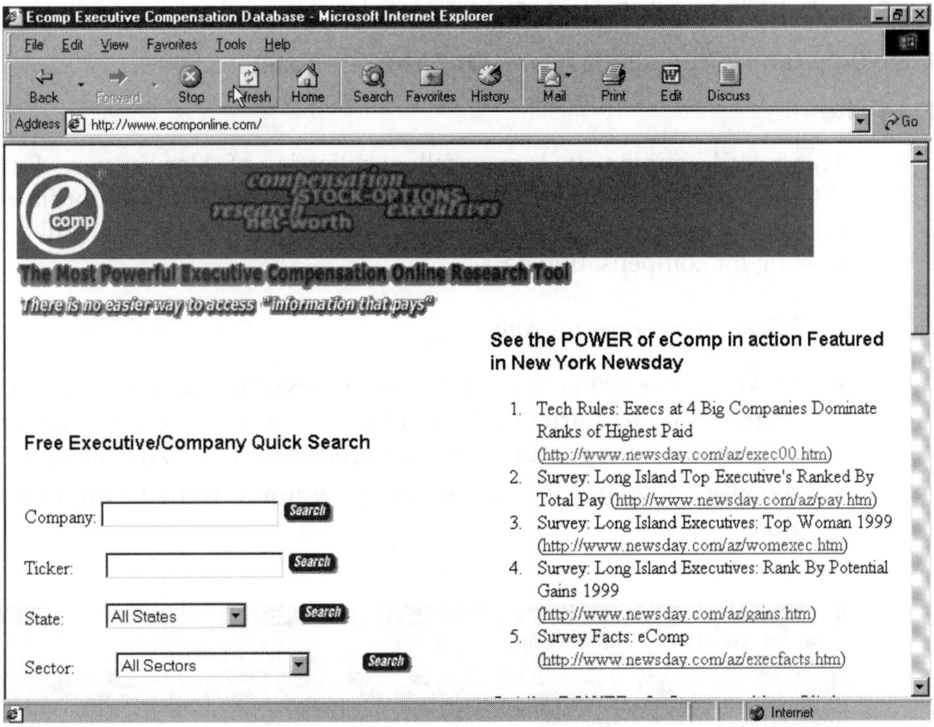

Exhibit 6.4 eComp Executive Compensation Database

The Institute of Management and Administration

www.ioma.com/zone/index.shtml

Free and Fee-based site

The Institute of Management and Administration (IOMA) was one of the first consulting firms to create a content-rich Internet site.

What can you expect to find?

- The site's "Salary Zone" contains titles of surveys contained in the orgranization's print publication *Report on Salary Surveys* (*RSS*), which reports on 10 to 12 salary surveys from a variety of industries.

- The Salary Zone also features a "Salary Survey" of the month, which is taken from *RSS*.

- Links are provided to each data source, such as a contributing trade association.

- Subscriptions to *RSS* are available online.

JobStar: California Job Search Guide

http://jobstar.org/tools/salary/sal-prof.htm   (Exhibit 6.5)

Free site

This award-winning site is an excellent collection of salary surveys for over 40 different industries. While JobStar is a career database for California job seekers, the information it compiles on salaries and job hunting is useful to anyone looking for compensation data.

What can you expect to find?

- Links to over 300 general and industry-specific salary surveys; while the emphasis is on salaries in California, many of the links are to national surveys that run the gamut from wine producers to auto mechanics
- Articles on job hunting, developing a resume, and a forum to ask questions

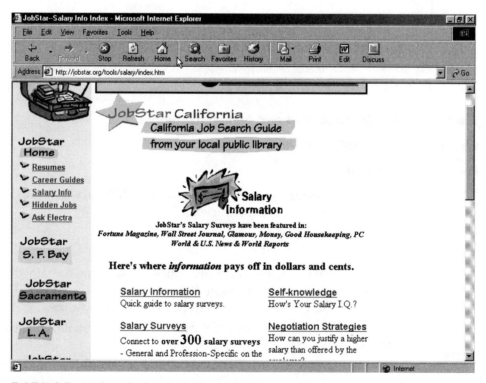

Exhibit 6.5 JobStar: California Job Search Guide
JobStar: California Job Search Guide (http://jobstar.org).

LivEdgar

www.gsionline.com

Fee-based site

The Securities and Exchange Commission mandates that publicly traded companies disclose the compensation of their chief executives, officers, and directors. Global Securities Inc. was one of the first companies to make searching the EDGAR database easy and cost effective, with its LivEdgar database.

What can you expect to find?

- LivEdgar's preformatted searches help researchers find examples of executive compensation tables while drafting documents for their clients' use. These "canned" searches are found on the site's "Research Library." Examples of preformatted searches involving compensation include: "Compensation Agreement" and "Compensation Committee Report."
- The "Executive/Summary Compensation Table" search allows users to search for compensation statistics by name, SIC codes, state, date, and keyword.
- Users can download the data directly into a spreadsheet.

Occupational Employment Statistics

http://stats.bls.gov/oeshome.htm

Free site

The U.S. Bureau of Labor Statistics provides the *Occupational Employment and Wage Estimates* in the form of an interactive database on the Net. Data is currently available for 1998 on a metropolitan, state, and national level. For each geographic level, employment and wage estimates are provided for each of the seven broad industry categories (managerial, professional, sales, clerical, service, agricultural, and production). Within each broad industry category are more specific subcategories. Earlier data is also available on the site.

What can you expect to find?

- Number of employed people within each occupation title, median, mean, and annual hourly wage

SalariesReview.com

www.salariesreview.com   (Exhibit 6.6)

Fee-based site

The Economic Research Institute (ERI) is a publisher of wage, salary, cost-of-living, human resource, and demographic information as it relates to employee pay. On a separate website the firm provides its SalariesReview.com, an interactive online database containing consensus data based on the OES data from the BLS and adjusted for online survey participation.

What can you expect to find?

- For $18 researchers can buy a report of "median," "low," and "high" wage or salary, along with an average "bonus" for any one of about 4,000 positions in any of 5,800 U.S. and Canadian locations.

- From ERI's home page (*www.erieri.com*) users can find a link to "ERI's Listing of Surveys and Sources: Listing of Available U.S. and Canadian Salary Surveys."

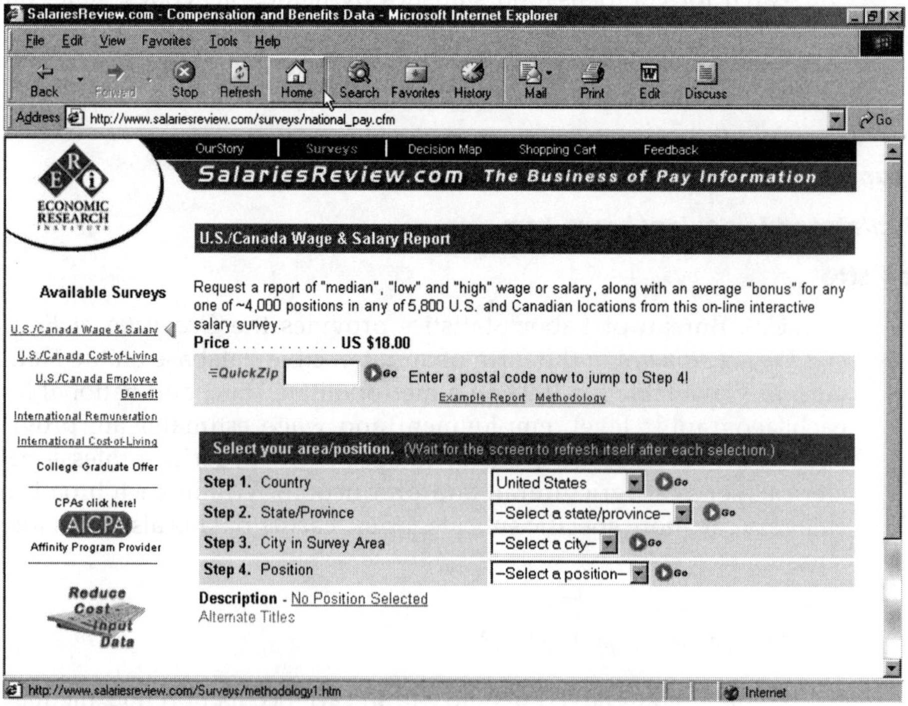

Exhibit 6.6   SalariesReview.com—Compensation and Benefits Data

Salary.com

www.salary.com (Exhibit 6.7)

Free site

The Salary Wizard, available at salary.com, is a free, "comprehensive salary tool enabling users to research salary ranges for thousands of job titles in a comprehensive set of career fields, sorted by occupation and region." The data is gathered from proprietary research and published reports. The Salary Wizard is also available on other websites, including AOL, jobs.com, Hoover's, Yahoo!, CareerCreations.com, Vault.com, WetFeet.com, Venture Vortex, postnet.com, College Recruiter, and BigJobBoard.com.

What can you expect to find?

- To find out what an electrician in Portland, Oregon, makes, from the initial "Select Job Category" option, select "Skilled and Trades," and then highlight "Oregon-Portland" from the "State/Metro" area box. A variety of job

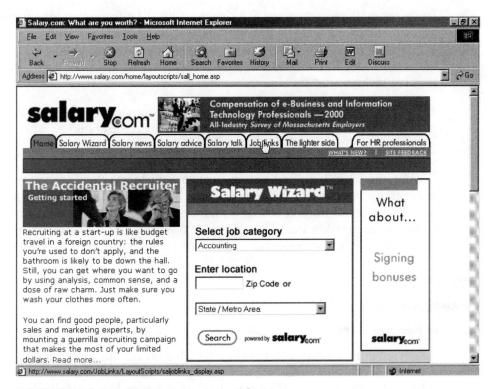

Exhibit 6.7 Salary.com: What are you worth?

descriptions will be retrieved. Select "Electrician III." The median base salary is $44,588.

- A "Total Cash Compensation" report is available for the same job category.
- Users have the ability to compare the same job in a different location or a related job in the same location.
- Links to related salary surveys are provided on the search results page.
- News and feature articles on compensation and workplace trends and issues are available.
- The site provides a compensation glossary and a Frequently Asked Questions list.

Trade Associations

http://info.asaenet.org/gateway/OnlineAssocSlist.html

www.associationcentral.com

Free and Fee-based sites

Trade associations often serve as a clearinghouse of information for a particular industry, therefore it is worthwhile to check an association's Web page. Trade associations survey members for compensation statistics, which the associations then compile, analyze, and sell to members and the general public.

Two websites aid the researcher in targeting a trade association:

1. The American Society for Association Executives "Gateway to Associations" (*http://info.asaenet.org/gateway/OnlineAssocSlist.html*)
2. Association Central (*www.associationcentral.com*)

Use the sites' keyword search functions to locate the appropriate trade association. While entire surveys may not be available for free on an association's website, portions of studies commonly are. If a trade association makes its salary surveys known to the public, it typically lists them under "publications," "research," or "reports."

Wage Web

www.wageweb.com

Free and Fee-based site

WageWeb is an online "salary service which provides information on over 170 benchmark positions." Researchers can access national data free of charge, and subscribers can access the salary survey information, broken down by geography, number of employees, and industry, for a nominal fee.

What can you expect to find?

- The salary surveys are organized in eight broad industry topics. Each industry contains anywhere from 9 to 30 benchmark positions. Each free, national survey contains the title, number of companies responding, mean average minimum salary, mean average salary, mean average maximum salary, and average bonus paid, if any.

BEST OF THE REST

CompGeo Online

www.compgeo.net   (Exhibit 6.8)

Fee-based site

CompGeo Online is a "Geographic Salary Survey Research site with forecasting options, best suited for salary and compensation survey research for a small number of jobs or job families." CompGeo Online, produced by the

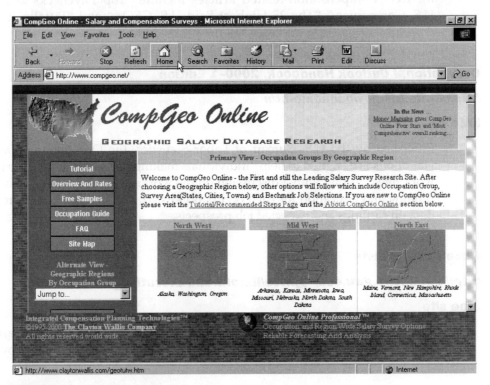

Exhibit 6.8 CompGeo Online
Copyright 2000 The Clayton Wallis Company, *www.claytonwallis.com.* All rights reserved. Used with permission.

Clayton Wallis Company, is a database of 1,000 salary survey benchmark jobs for 23 occupations groups. A number of reports are available from the interactive website, and are priced between $39 and $329.

The CompGeo Online Standard Reports are provided for each industry/sector breakout and a particular area/job. The report includes projected mean and median, low, and high individual wage and salary estimates, estimated competitive salary ranges, quartile-based range, tercile-based range, and salary differentials for 10 U.S. regions. A variety of more detailed reports are available in Adobe PDF format and delivered in secure password protected files.

Forbes

www.forbes.com

Free site

The *Forbes* website provides hundred of articles from current and past issues for free. Compensation-related articles include "Top Paychecks at 50 Big U.S. Companies," "The 25 Highest-Paid U.S. CEOs," and "Pitfalls of Stock Options."

Occupational Outlook Handbook, 2000–1 Edition

http://stats.bls.gov/ocohome.htm

Free site

Published by the U.S. Bureau of Labor Statistics, the Occupational Outlook Handbook is designed to help "individuals making decisions about their future work lives." Along with a discussion on the working conditions and necessary training and education for each occupation listed, the handbook also provides data on earnings and expected job prospects.

Price's List of Lists

http://gwis2.circ.gwu.edu/~gprice/listof.htm#Executive_Compensation

Free site

This site is compiled by Gary Price, of the Gelman Library at George Washington University. Links to executive compensation–related lists are provided.

Examples include "What Lawyers Earn" from *Law Journal Extra* and "Gaming Industry's Top 59 Compensated CEO's."

Valuation Resources.com

www.valuationresources.com

Free site

The link "Industry Resources Reports" leads researchers to lists of sources of compensation surveys by SIC code.

William M. Mercer

www.wmmercer.com

Fee-based site

Unfortunately, abstracts of Mercer's well-known compensation surveys are not available on their website, but researchers can purchase the compensation surveys online. The firm also provides its "MarketPricer Online," a survey analysis tool that lets users query, view, import, and export survey statistics. It is important to note that the Mercer reports are available only to "individuals responsible for administering corporate compensation, benefits, and/or human resources" and are "not available to the general public."

CHAPTER 7

Mergers and Acquisitions

Jan Davis Tudor

The Internet has made access to merger and acquisition (M&A) data so much easier than in the past. Databases that were once only available through a direct dial-up service with a difficult search procedure have now been restructured to take advantage of the popular graphics-based nature of the Internet. It is important to note that not all information on the Net is free, especially in the case of M&A data. Most of the M&A products listed in our "First and Foremost" section require a password and a subscription fee.

M&A data is sought after for a number of reasons:

- Business appraisers need to find market data for companies similar to the one they are valuing.

- When looking for a possible buyer for a client's business, intermediaries need to find out what companies have already made similar purchases.

- Journalists who follow the current M&A environment need to keep abreast of current M&A announcements and transactions on a daily basis.

- Lawyers like to look at the SEC filings when drafting agreements between two parties of a transaction.

All sites are presented in alphabetical order. The sites listed in the "First and Foremost" section of this chapter are those that the authors have found to be reliable, well organized, and rich sources of information. Sites offering all or part of the data for free are considered more desirable than sites offering similar data for a fee. "Best of the Rest" sites may focus on a niche area, be fee only, or have limited navigation and output features.

FIRST AND FOREMOST

BIZCOMPS

Available online from Nvst (*http://bizcomps.nvst.com*)   (Exhibit 7.1) and Business Valuation Resources (*www.bvmarketdata.com*)

Fee-based sites

BIZCOMPS is a database of financial data on the sales of small businesses. Business intermediary Jack Sanders began the print version of the BIZCOMPS studies around 1979 because he saw the need for a centralized source of data for the sales of businesses valued under $1 million. Sanders gathers the data from full-time certified business brokers and intermediaries.

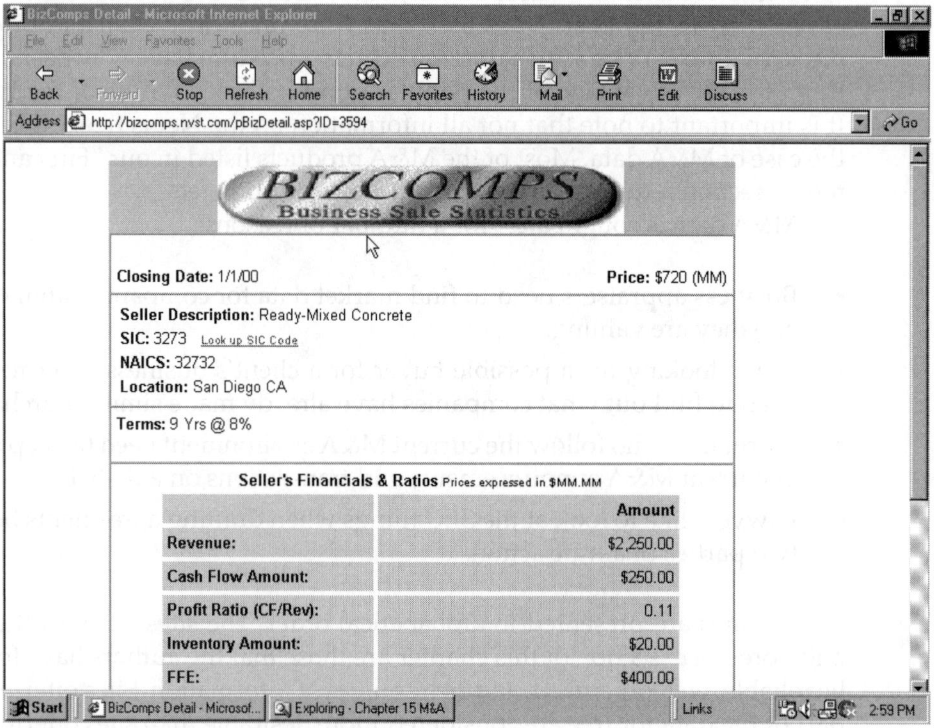

Exhibit 7.1 BIZCOMPS Business Sale Statistics from NVST.com

BIZCOMPS is a unique database in that it contains the multiples and terms of small business sales. The average sales price in the database is $858,774. Typically this data is difficult to find, since in most cases buyers and sellers are not required to disclose the information. Today the database contains 4,400 asset sales dating back to 1979 and is updated three times a year.

What can you expect to find?

- Each transaction contains ratios such as sale price to gross sales, sale price to sellers' cash flow, and sales compared to sellers' cash flow as well as the value of inventory, the price of the sale, and the state where it occurred.
- BIZCOMPS is searchable by Standard Industrial Classification (SIC) code, North American Industry Classification System (NAICS), sales size, price, geographical area, and keyword.
- The name of the target and the acquiring company are not provided because neither buyers nor sellers are required to disclose that information.

Business Valuation Market Data

www.BVMarketData.com   (Exhibit 7.2)

Fee-based site

BVMarketData is a website that includes several databases of financial details of completed sales of businesses.

Pratt's Stats is a new database since 1997, and it is a welcome newcomer because it provides far more information on private transactions than was ever available previously. Pratt's Stats is the official database of the International Business Brokers Association and contains data on transactions that has been provided to the database's founder, Shannon Pratt, by a number of contributing business brokers and intermediaries.

What can you expect to find?

- The Pratt's Stats database provides 70 data fields for each transaction including summary balance sheets and income statements for the companies involved, as well as the terms of each transaction. Other data include SIC and NAICS codes, company location, employees, time in business, dates and prices listed and sold, and noncompete and employment agreement terms and price allocation. The publishers compute eight valuation multiples for each transaction.
- The database is searchable by multiple criteria and transactions may be downloaded or data exported to an Excel spreadsheet for analysis.

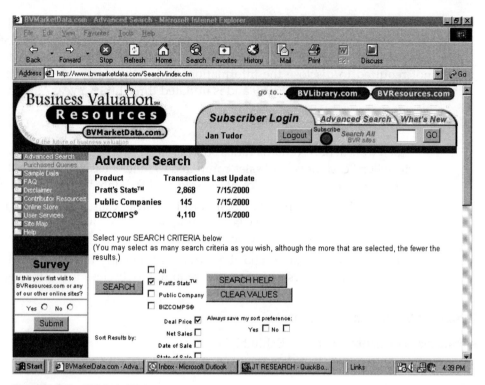

Exhibit 7.2   BVMarketData.com

Pratt's Stats™ is the official business-sales database of the International Business Brokers Association. Used with permission from Business Valuation Resources, LLC, 7412 SW Beaverton-Hillsdale Hwy, Suite 106, Portland, OR 97225; ph: (503) 291-7963; fax: (503) 291-7955. Online (*www. BVMarketData.com*™) and print/software subscriptions to Pratt's Stats™ are available.

- So far the database contains 3200 transactions and in the future it will increase in size, popularity, and usefulness.

- Pratt's Stats Mid-Market Public Companies is a new portion of the database started in July 2000. It contains data similar to that on Pratt's Stats private company database for sales of public companies with a deal value under $100 million.

- BIZCOMPS, described earlier, is also available at BVMarketData.com. BIZCOMPS and Pratt's Stats may be searched simultaneously by SIC and NAICS codes, and data printed out or exported to an Excel spreadsheet, either together or separately.

- *Mergerstat/Shannon Pratt's Control Premium Studies* are a new part of the BVMarketData website. Formerly available only in print form, this database of completed transactions compares acquisition price with former public market trading price, including public prices at several points in time before the acquisition announcement. A feature not included in the prior print versions is classification of the transaction as financial, horizontal integration, vertical integration, or conglomerate. The data on the website includes 1998 through the present.

Corporate Growth Deal Retriever

www.nvst.com/onlineDB/pnvDB/pnvDatabases.asp

Fee-based site

The Corporate Growth Deal Retriever contains M&A transaction data derived from the *Corporate Growth Weekly Report.* The Quality Services Company in Santa Barbara, California, originally published the report; however, Nvst.com purchased it in early 2000 and now makes the data available in electronic format via the new database, the Corporate Growth Deal Retriever. The database contains over 1,000 middle-market transactions and is updated weekly.

What can you expect to find?

- Summaries of new offers, takeover speculations, and market summaries of current mergers, acquisitions, divestitures, joint ventures, and initial public offerings
- All purchase price ratios, historical financial data, balance sheet information on buyer and seller, and a description of each transaction

The *Daily Deal*

www.thedailydeal.com   (Exhibit 7.3)

Free and Fee-based site

The *Daily Deal* is a daily newspaper, published Monday to Friday, that focuses on mergers and acquisitions. Researchers can find news of recent transactions, feature articles, and special reports. The publication gathers and compiles data from over 12 vendors, compiled from 16 or 17 vendors, such as Mergerstat and Done Deals.

Approximately 40 people write for the publication, and all have either industry beats, such as telecommunications or utilities, or deal segment beats, such as private equity or venture capital. The *Daily Deal* also has reporters in different regions where M&A is expanding, such as Europe and Asia.

Exhibit 7.3 The DailyDeal.com

What can you expect to find?

- The daily "Scoreboard," with useful charts, graphs, tables, a daily roster of transactions, "Multiples Day," and "Pricing Day"
- Special reports such as compensation surveys of dealmakers
- News about industry "movers and shakers"

Done Deals

http://donedeals.nvst.com/checklogin.asp   (Exhibit 7.4)

Fee-based site

John Bailey and the World M&A Network in Washington, D.C., created Done Deals. However, Nvst.com purchased the database in 1999 and makes it available via its website. Done Deals' specialty is providing data on midmarket transactions, or those deals valued between $1 million and $100 million. Approximately 50 percent of the deals are under $10 million and 50 percent are

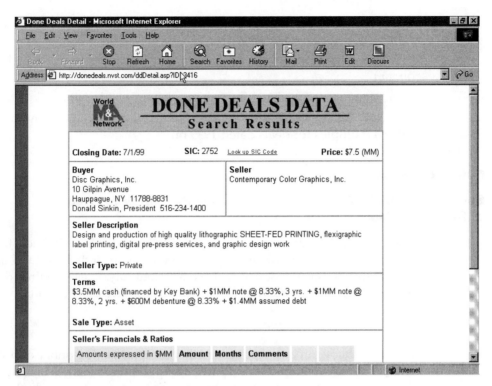

Exhibit 7.4   Done Deals Data from NVST.com

over $10 million. Approximately 50 percent of the selling companies are privately owned.

Database information is extracted from a variety of SEC filings, making the product an excellent source on transactions involving public acquiring companies and private acquired companies.

Currently the database contains over 4,000 transactions dating back to 1994. The database is searchable by closing date, SIC code, price, buyer and/or seller name, keywords in the seller's business description, type of target (private, public, subsidiary, and asset or stock sale, or both). Yearly subscriptions that allow for unlimited searching are available from Nvst.com.

What can you expect to find?

- Purchase price ratios, such as price/earnings, price/cash flow from operations, price/revenue, price/assets and price/stockholders equity for each deal

- The ability to create regression and *r*-squared charts based on search results or user-designed criteria

- Company contacts (name of the executive handling the deal, address, phone)

- Price, terms, and sources of financing

- Price/EBITDA (earnings before interest, taxes, depreciation, and amortization) multiples for deals dated 1999 on

EDGAR Databases

Several sites make EDGAR documents available either for free or for a small fee:

EDGAR filings are the disclosure documents filed with the SEC. Publicly traded companies are required to disclose specific information to the SEC, and in the past few years have been required to do so electronically. These required disclosure documents, called EDGAR filings, are a great source of M&A information.

What can you expect to find?

- When a public company acquires another company, either public or private, and the transaction represents a particular amount of business in relation to the acquirer's current business, the acquiring company must disclose the terms of the deal to the SEC. Typically the particulars of the deal, including the acquired company's financial data, is included in Form 8-K.

10K Wizard
www.10kwizard.com   (Exhibits 7.5 and 7.6)
Free site

10K Wizard is a free source of EDGAR filings and is a favorite among those who use these documents for business research. The site's EDGAR database can be searched by keywords, phrases, company name, industry segment, SIC code, form group, form type, ticker, and date. For instance, to locate transactions in the motor vehicle parts and accessories industry, one could search by SIC code 3714, limit the search to 8-K–related forms, and add the keyword "acquisition."

Free EDGAR
www.freeedgar.com
Free site

Free EDGAR is also a free source of EDGAR filings. The site's EDGAR database is searchable by keyword, company name, ticker, SIC code, date, location, and SEC form type. An added feature of Free EDGAR is the ability to view and

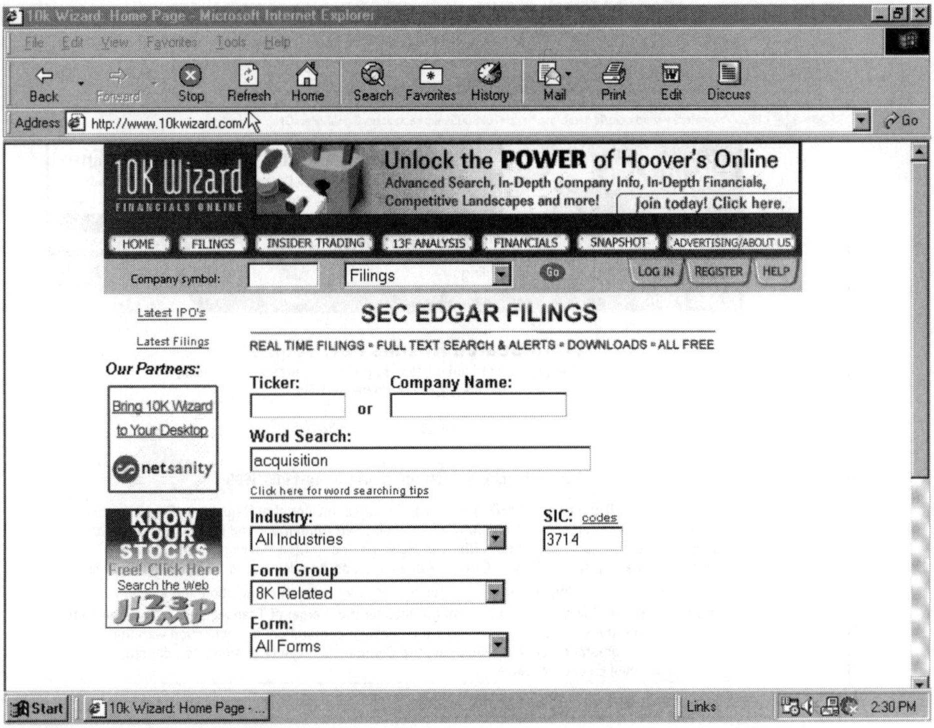

Exhibit 7.5   10K Wizard Home Page

print a document in RTF as well as select and download specific sections of a
filing. That can come in very handy when a filing is 600 pages.

LivEdgar
www.gsionline.com   (Exhibit 7.7)
Fee-based site

Global Securities Information Inc.'s (GSI) LivEdgar is a fee-based source of
EDGAR documents. However, the fee is very reasonable and is offered as a
pay-as-you-go system. LivEdgar also provides an optional custom-billing format that allows users to track their research by client or project codes. Monthly
or yearly subscriptions are available.

Researchers pay to use this database because they can perform sophisticated searches with it. Furthermore, financials included in forms such as the
8-K can be downloaded directly into a spreadsheet. In addition, researchers
often use the preformatted searches created by the GSI staff to find documents
similar to the ones they are creating, such as one of the many legal documents
necessary between the buyer and the seller of a company.

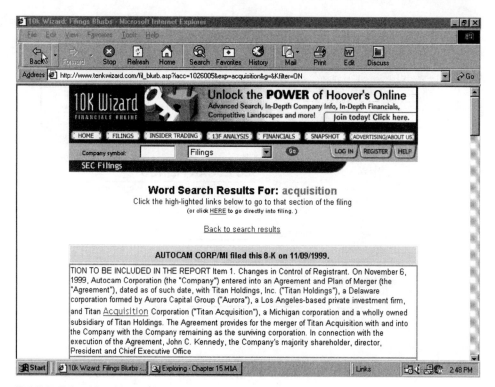

Exhibit 7.6   10K Wizard: Search Results for Acquisition

Global Securities Information's '33 Act Deals Database

www.gsionline.com   (Exhibit 7.8)

Fee-based site

This database is an excellent source of all registered public offerings from 1996 forward and is used most often for registration and prospectus research. Most researchers use this database for precedent language, comparable deals, and exhibits.

Registrations and final prospectus are searchable by a variety of indexed fields, such as keywords in the deal description, offering price, underwriter, security type, date, form type, and status.

What can you expect to find?

- Specific registrations or deals
- The most recent original, amended, and final initial public offerings
- The ability to create rankings based on final prospectus information
- Abstract reports

Exhibit 7.7 LivEdgar Mergers & Acquisitions Research Library
Courtesy of Global Securities Information, Inc.

Global Securities Information's Mergers & Acquisitions Database

www.gsionline.com (Exhibit 7.9)

Fee-based site

The Mergers & Acquisitions database contains transactions derived from original SEC source documents. This database has an intuitive interface and is reasonably priced. Data from deals derived from a variety of form types including 14D-1s from July 1996 to the present; S-4s from July 1997 to the present; F-4s from July 1999 to the present; 8-Ks from November 1999 to the present; 6-Ks from January 2000 to the present; and all Forms TOs.

What can you expect to find?

- More than 70 types of transactions
- The ability to search by dozens of options, such as target financials, SIC code(s), transaction value, and geographic region

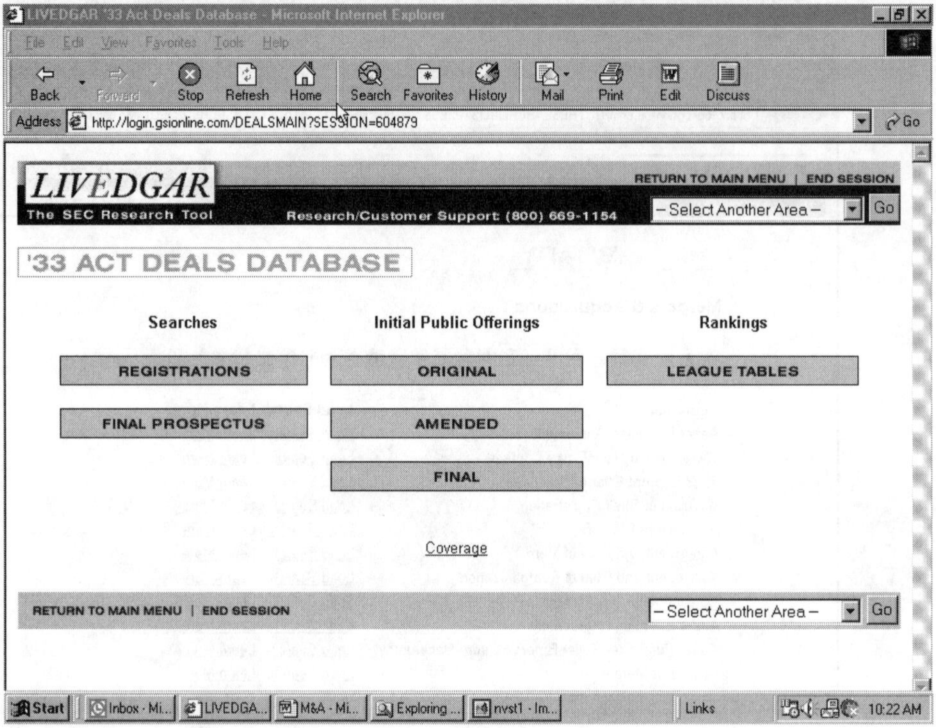

Exhibit 7.8 LivEdgar '33 Acts Deals Database
Courtesy of Global Securities Information, Inc.

- Concise summaries of each deal, including attorneys, financial advisors, and fees
- The ability to create custom league tables

Mergerstat (Database)

Available from .XLS (*www.xls.com*), Factset (*www.factset.com*), Lexis-Nexis (*www.lexis-nexis.com*), and Bloomberg (*www.bloomberg.com*)

Fee-based sites

While Mergerstat has gained its reputation by being an authoritative source of M&A data during the past 35 years, the database came on the market in 1995. Mergerstat is a division of investment bank and financial advisory firm Houlihan Lokey Howard & Zukin. The company's analysts gather M&A information from SEC filings, investment banks, press releases, news sources, and

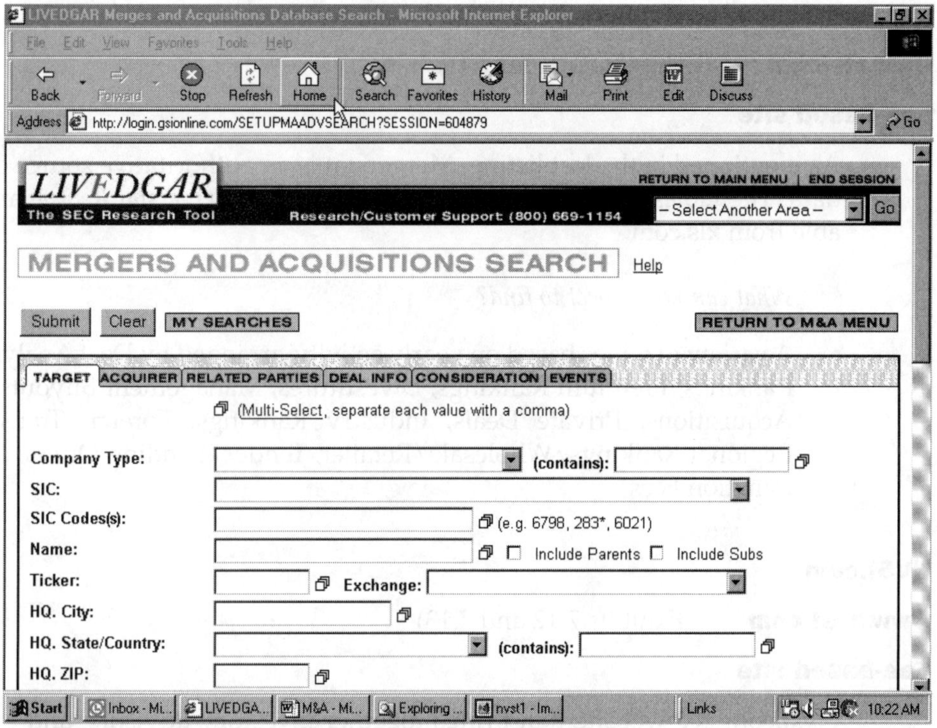

Exhibit 7.9 LivEdgar Mergers and Acquisitions Database Search
Courtesy of Global Securities Information, Inc.

professional contacts. Only those transactions valued at $1 million and over are included in the database, which is updated daily.

The Mergerstat database is a much-welcomed source of M&A data because it provides a more cost-effective way to access M&A data than through Thomson Financial Securities Data. It contains deals involving both private and public companies. Mergerstat recently acquired a British company, CorpFin, which is an excellent source of data of non-U.S. transactions. This acquisition will greatly enhance the Mergerstat database.

What can you expect to find?

- Data on deals dating back to 1992
- Data on cross-border transactions that involve U.S. companies
- The ability to create reports of deals based on a variety of data points, such as valuation multiples, premiums paid, seller financials, announcement and closing dates, and SIC code

Mergerstat Review Tables

www.xls.com   (Exhibits 7.10 and 7.11)

Fee-based site

As mentioned in the last listing, Mergerstat is an authoritative source of M&A data. The tables published in the renowned print *Mergerstat Review* are available from xls.com.

What can you expect to find?

- A variety of tables based on yearly activity, arranged by Deal Analysis, P/E Rankings, Premium Rankings, Divestitures, Management Buyouts, Public Acquisitions, Private Deals, Industry Rankings, Foreign Transactions, Regional Rankings/Wholesale/Retailer, Tender/Pending Offers, and Termination Fees

NVST.com

www.nvst.com   (Exhibits 7.12 and 7.13)

Fee-based site

Nvst.com is a website that brings together investors, advisors, and entrepreneurs of privately held businesses. The content of the site is focused on all aspects of the life cycle of a business, from funding to selling. Nvst.com is a clearinghouse of M&A-related information and can be applauded for its efforts and success in providing M&A data to researchers.

What can you expect to find?

- Three M&A databases, Done Deals, BIZCOMPS, and the Corporate Growth Deal Retriever, by using the NVST Multi-Database Search feature. The initial search, which determines the number of deals found in each database, is free. Searches can be created by SIC code, transaction date, sale price, and/or revenue.

  After reviewing the search results, searchers can link directly to the databases that contain the deals that match the search criteria. Researchers must be paid subscribers to the database in order to retrieve the full record for each deal.

- Nvst.com also provides links to M&A-related organizations, such as the Association for Corporate Growth and the International Merger and Acquisition Professionals, as well as a conference calendar. In addition, it provides sample issues and subscriptions to publications such as *Fair*

Search Criteria:
Target SIC: 7372
Base Equity Price: 5 to 50
Announced Date: 1/1/98 - 10/4/00
Enterprise Value/EBITDA: Not Null

Announced	Closed	Seller	Buyer	Deal Size / Equity Value ($mm)	Enterprise Value ($mm)	Target Primary SIC	Target Business Description	Target Revenue LTM ($mm)	EBIT LTM	EBITDA LTM	Method of Payment	P/E	Price/Book Value	Price/Revenue	EV/EBIT	EV/EBITDA	EV/Revenue
21-Jul-00		LibertyOne Ltd	CyberSentry Inc	38.59	38.59	7372	Provides Internet content and technology	14.03	-21.60	-14.16	Stock	-1.8	0.79	2.75	-1.79	-2.73	2.75
17-Jul-00		CFI ProServices Inc	Harland (John H.) Co	37.88	138.68	7372	Provides financial software	120.04	-10.43	0.10	Cash	-2.4	-1.06	0.32	-13.30	1386.80	1.16
17-Jul-00	23-Aug-00	Concentrex Inc	Harland (John H.) Co	39.24	112.72	7372	Develops software for financial institutions; develops customer relationship management	119.04	-10.43	0.96	Cash	-2.5	-1.10	0.33	-10.81	117.42	0.94
15-May-00		ODND Inc	ePresence Inc	29.45	29.33	7372	Develops software solutions; eMobility, wireless and custom application development companies	11.68	2.27	2.46	Combo	13.2	13.21	2.52	12.92	11.92	2.51
11-May-00		Mainbrace Corp	BSQUARE Corp / BuzzCompany.com	18.10	19.12	7372	Develops software products for pocket Web telephone, Wireless MSN Web, and...	3.13	-1.56	-1.49	Combo	-11.5	62.41	5.78	-12.26	-12.83	6.11
10-May-00		Multex.com Inc	OUInc	22.32	22.23	7372	Provides e-Community Internet products/services	2.88	-0.48	-0.42	Combo	-45.6	16.78	7.75	-46.31	-52.93	7.72
13-Apr-00	17-May-00	Medifor Inc	Allscripts Inc	33.34	35.92	7372	Provides clinical software for physicians; provides business-to-business infrastructure	1.09	-1.38	-1.29	Stock	-23.8	151.55	30.59	-26.03	-27.84	32.95
27-Mar-00		Muscato Corp	Optio Software Inc	33.00	33.98	7372	Provides software and services	6.95	-0.69	-0.57	Combo	-78.8	84.62	4.75	-49.25	-59.61	4.85
09-Mar-00		Premia Corp / Universal Value	StarBase Corp	23.83	23.26	7372	Provides life cycle management solutions	5.31	0.13	0.22	Stock	184.2	15.68	4.49	178.92	105.73	4.38
08-Mar-00		Network / Premier Softwar	Netcentives Inc	20.70	24.76	7372	Provides payment card applications; retailers	0.36	-0.34	-0.26	Combo	-32.9	21.34	57.50	-72.82	-95.23	68.76
25-Feb-00	03-May-00	Technologies In	Active Software Inc	5.00	4.87	7372	Develops e-commerce integration software plug-ins; develops interactive graphics and computer-a...	1.51	-1.21	-1.20	Combo	-4.0	-2.02	3.31	-4.02	-4.06	3.23
18-Feb-00	19-May-00	Graphsoft Inc	Nemetschek AG	29.17	28.09	7372	design software	8.97	1.61	2.71	Cash	25.6	2.65	3.25	17.45	10.37	3.13
17-Feb-00	15-May-00	SDR Technologie National Informa / OUInc	Consortium Inc	19.96	22.74	7372	Develops electronic government applications; services and licenses...	2.63	-0.85	-0.77	Stock	-20.3	-9.74	7.59	-26.75	-29.53	8.65
21-Jan-00	31-Jan-00	WebWizard Inc	Grace Developmen Corp	7.08	7.08	7372	software for the creation and management...	0.00	-0.03	-0.03	Stock	-210.3	-70.80		-236.00	-236.00	-236.00
20-Jan-00	11-Feb-00	Aller Inc	Active Software Inc	32.10	32.65	7372	Web sites enterprise application; develops software for the banking and financ... industries	1.61	-3.08	-1.14	Combo	-10.1	-30.87	19.94	-10.60	-28.64	20.26
17-Jan-00	21-Jan-00	Image Info Inc	QRS Corp	47.67	47.89	7372	Provides digital imaging software; photography services to the retail	7.03	-0.07	0.04	Combo	-285.4	140.21	6.78	-684.14	1197.25	6.81
28-Dec-99	28-Apr-00	ORTIO Corp / USA I	CE Software Holdings Inc	9.66	13.71	7372	Designs, develops, and sells a comp... customer interaction solution for e...	2.10	-4.15	-3.94	Stock	-2.0	-1.50	4.60	-3.30	-3.48	6.53
15-Dec-99	12-Jan-00	Pivotpoint Inc	Maptics Inc	48.00	107.38	7372	Develops enterprise solutions for t...; manufacturing and distribution indu...	24.18	2.16	2.83	Cash	-22.4	-0.68	1.99	49.71	37.94	4.44
03-Dec-99	22-Mar-00	Analogy Inc	Avant! Corp	24.05	24.67	7372	Develops high-performance software; Provides library for top-down design; Provides solutions to enable interm	25.97	-1.34	2.40	Cash	-11.9	5.91	0.93	-18.41	10.28	0.95
19-Nov-99	03-Feb-00	ConnectInc.com / OUCo	Calico Commerce Inc	46.10	41.50	7372	electronic commerce; Develops, markets, implements, and enterprise management software desi...	6.30	-14.60	-14.06	Cash	-3.1	9.43	7.32	-2.84	-2.95	6.59
09-Nov-99	09-Nov-99	Design Data Systems Corp	ASA Internation Ltd	5.00	6.15	7372	enterprise management companies; develops, markets and supports core service-oriented application development to	7.12	0.60	0.76	Cash	12.4	-6.58	0.70	10.25	8.09	0.86
04-Nov-99	13-Apr-00	ObjectShare Inc	StarBase Corp	7.08	6.44	7372	client/server/Web computing market	15.32	-5.20	-4.47	Stock	-1.3	-7.61	0.46	-1.24	-1.44	0.42

Copyright © 2000, Mergerstat.

Exhibit 7.10 Mergerstat Sample Report from XLS.com

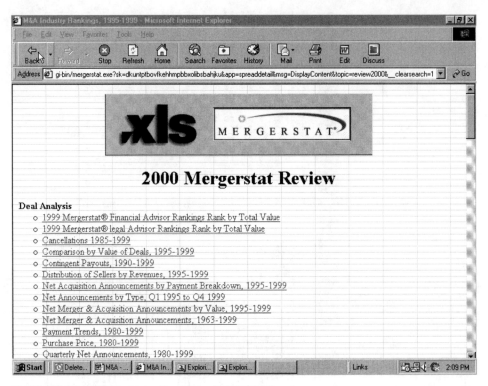

Exhibit 7.11   M&A Industry Rankings, 1995–1999

Market Reporter, M&A Today, and *Mergers & Acquisitions: The Dealmaker's Journal.*

SNL Securities

www.snl.com

Fee-based site

SNL Securities are experts in the financial services industries, and their website provides information on M&A relating to banks, thrifts, financial services companies, real estate investment companies, and insurance companies. Those interested in the buying and selling of companies within the financial services industries will find this site useful.

What can you expect to find?

- Recent headlines from SNL publications *Specialty Lender Mergers & Acqui-*

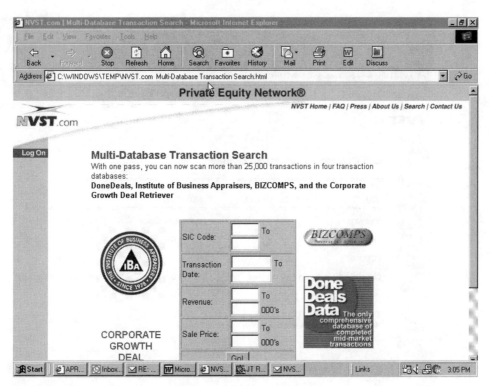

Exhibit 7.12   NVST.com: Multi-Database Transaction Search

sitions and *Securities and Investments Mergers & Acquisitions* as well as information about the company's M&A databases

- Charts such as "Top Specialty Lender Asset Sales for the 2nd Quarter 2000 Ranked by Receivables Sold"
- Data-filled press releases

Thomson Financial Securities Data Company Global Worldwide M&A Database

Available from Thomson Financial (*www.tfsd.com* and *www.thomsondirect.com*), Dialog (*www.dialog.com*), Lexis/Nexis (*www.lexis-nexis.com*), and Data Downlink (*www.xls.com*)

Fee-based sites

This database, commonly referred to as the SDC database, is the most comprehensive source of M&A transaction data. It is the only publicly available source of deals dating back to 1979, although the database's true comprehensiveness begins with its coverage in the late 1980s and early 1990s. Currently

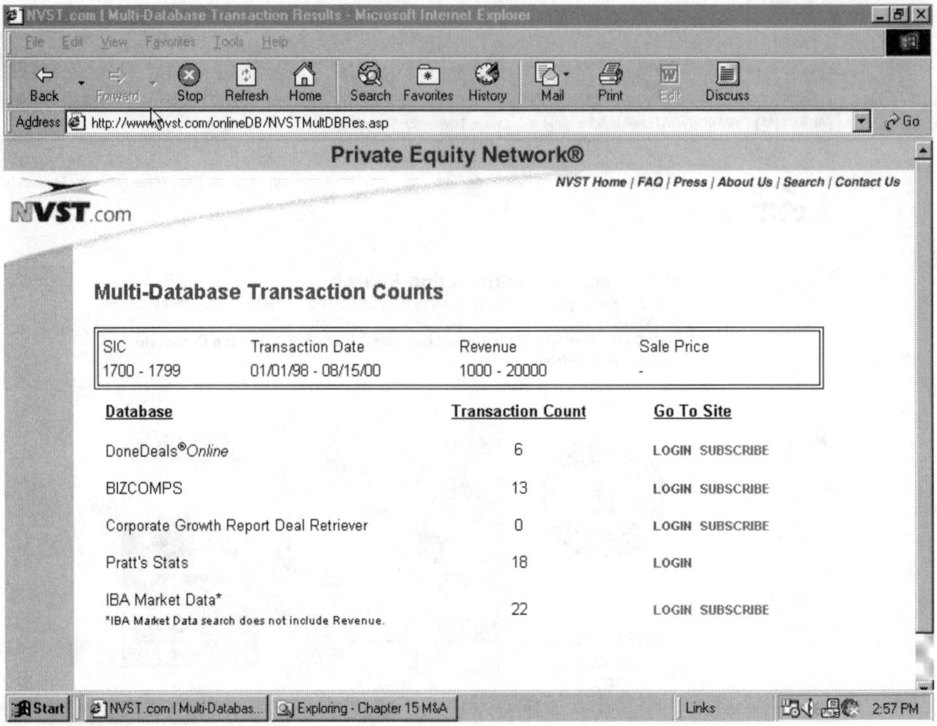

Exhibit 7.13   NVST.com: Multi-Database Transaction Counts

the database contains data on more than 273,000 transactions and includes only those deals valued at over $1 million. One drawback of the SDC database is that it can be very expensive to use. We recommend that users attend SDC training classes or call the company's technical support line before initiating a search.

In today's global economy, it would be foolish to think that deals outside of the U.S. are not important. In fact, cross-border deals are increasing at a rapid pace. The SDC database offers more information on non-U.S. deals than any other source.

What can you expect to find?

- SDC records as much information as it can on each deal. The database can be searched by approximately 1,200 different data items, such as target and acquirer business descriptions, deal terms, stock premiums paid, and financial and legal advisor fees. Users can create specific searches, such as "all of the deals within SIC code 1711 between 1997 and 2000 that were for a majority interest, with a deal value of over $10 million and with EBITDA multiples available." In addition to SIC codes, SDC has created more detailed codes for subsectors within the high-technology industry.

XLS.com

www.xls.com

Fee-based site

XLS, a data aggregator, is a service of the Data Downlink company. XLS provides access to dozens of databases containing quantitative business and investment information from a variety of content providers. Researchers searching on a database provided through XLS can download the content directly into a spreadsheet.

What can you expect to find?

- Mergerstat (see listing in this chapter)
- Thomson Financial Securities Data Worldwide M&A Database (see listing in this chapter)
- The Carson Group and the Vickers Stock Research Corporation databases, which provide ownership information on public companies
- A variety of databases containing industry publications and market research reports
- Company databases, such as Graham & Whiteside, Harris InfoSource™, and CorpTech, which are excellent sources for putting together buyers' and sellers' lists
- Portal B, a database of 8,500 business-oriented sites hand-picked by information professionals, linked with XLS's fee-based content

BEST OF THE REST

American Society of Association Executives' Gateway

http://info.asaenet.org/gateway/OnlineAssocSlist.html

Free site

Trade associations often publish buyer's guides of and for their members. These guides can be excellent sources when putting together a buyer's or seller's list because they contain detailed descriptions of companies that participate within a particular industry. The American Society of Association Executives (ASAE) site is a great place to start looking for an industry's trade association because it provides links to over 6,500 member associations.

Carl UnCover

www.carl.org

Free and Fee-based site (free to search)

Carl UnCover is a database of over 18,000 journals in a variety of subjects. Researchers can use the database to find articles on topics relating to M&A, because journals such as the *Harvard Business Review* and *Institutional Investor* are indexed. In addition, UnCover serves as an alerting and document delivery service. Documents are ordered online and are either faxed within the hour or retrieved from member libraries. Subscribers also can set up an alert service that informs them of the table of contents of a new edition or articles on a defined subject.

Commscan

www.commscan.com/home.asp

Free and Fee-based site

This provider of M&A data furnishes a current table of 144A Underwriter Rankings on its website.

DLJ Direct

www.dljdirect.com/dljd/qnnewsma.htm

Free and Fee-based site

DLJ Direct is a Donaldson Lufkin & Jenrette company, and its website provides the latest headlines on mergers and acquisitions. The news stories are from Reuters.

International Business Brokers Association

www.ibba.org

Free site

The International Business Brokers Association (IBBA) set up a database of seller profiles on its website, which is searchable by geographic region, revenue, and type of business. A profile is provided for each of the companies retrieved from the search results. Each profile contains a description of the business, geographic region, SIC code, revenues, adjusted profit, asking price, legal structure, and number of employees. Those interested in the business are asked to contact the IBBA for more information.

Kagan and Associates

www.kagan.com/mma/megadeals_page.html

Free and Fee-based site

Kagan and Associates are industry experts on the media and telecommunications industries and provide news on media-related deals.

M&A Source

www.masource.org/news.asp

Free and Fee-based site

The M&A Source is a division of the IBBA and calls itself "the world's largest International Organization of experienced, dedicated Merger and Acquisition Intermediaries representing the Middle Market." While much of the information on the site is for members only, the public can search a database of buyer and seller profiles and access M&A-related news and articles.

Merger Market

www.mergermarket.com

Free site

Merger Market is a London-based source of European deal data. It provides current and archived deal news stories, a database of European transactions valued over £10 million, league tables, and lists of businesses for sale by company, sector, and/or geographic area.

Merger Network

www.mergernetwork.com

Free site

The Merger Network claims to be "the web's best source of merger and acquisition leads." Companies for sale are listed by region, industry, and business size. A detailed business description is provided for each company listed;

however, additional information carries a $20 fee. The site's "M&A Topic of the Month" features editorials on topics such as M&A insurance, and "Today's M&A News" provides daily Reuters news stories.

Mergers-r-us.com

www.mergers-r-us.com

Free site

This site provides good descriptions of types of mergers, such as reverse merger and traditional public shells.

Mergerstat

www.mergerstat.com   (Exhibit 7.14)

Free site

The Mergerstat Web page contains several free reports: "Total Number of Deals Back to 1930," "Top 10 Deals for 2000," "Top 10 Industry Rankings Year to Date," "Top Financial Advisors 2000," and "Top Legal Advisors 2000." In addition, the site offers a daily "M&A Update" that provides daily news on U.S. deals that have a value disclosed and international deals valued at over $100 million.

Powerize

www.powerize.com

Free and Fee-based site

Search Powerize for news and magazine articles on acquisitions by broad industry categories. Many articles are free, others cost around $2.50. Users must register with the site.

Thomas Register of American Manufacturers

www.thomasregister.com

Free site

Thomas Register of American Manufacturers is an established directory of manufacturers in the U.S. Its online version, Thomas Register Online, is free but utilizes a registration and password program. The register is an excellent site to use when putting together buyers' or sellers' lists of manufacturing companies.

Exhibit 7.14   Mergerstat Free Reports

The database, currently containing information on over 76,000 companies, is searchable by company name, product, or service.

Thomson Financial Securities Data

www.tfsd.com

Fee-based site

Thomson Financial Securities Data (TFSD) provides a lot of M&A-related data on their website, such as news and rankings. The news is pulled from TFSD publications, such as *IDD* magazine, and is archived back to January 1999. Not only can you search the current and archived news by region, but you can limit by geographic region, such as Latin America. Another useful feature of the TFSD website is the "Deals and Rankings" section, where tables such as "Top M&A Deals and Managers for July 2000" and "Worldwide M&A Activity First Half 2000" can be found.

Webmergers.com

www.webmergers.com

Free site

Webmergers.com "is the only dedicated source of data, analysis and services for buyers and sellers of web-related properties." The site provides not only a listing service for buyers and sellers of Web properties but also articles on "who is buying," "what are they buying," and "where are they buying." A free weekly newsletter, the Web M&A Update, is available and contains articles such as "Valuations Overview." Users can sign up for the free weekly "Update of Web M&A News & Analysis," which is delivered via e-mail.

World M&A Network

www.worldm-anetwork.com

Free site

World M&A Network site is updated daily, with subscribers receiving listings of companies for sale, merger candidates, and corporate buyers. Data is organized by SIC code, company size, and geographic region.

CHAPTER 8

Intellectual Property

Eva M. Lang

The concept of intellectual capital is bandied about on talk shows, in business magazines, and in the boardrooms of corporate America. Thomas A. Stewart in his book *Intellectual Capital—the New Wealth of Nations* defines intellectual capital as "intellectual material—knowledge, information, intellectual property, experience—that can be put to use to create wealth." Starting in the 1990s, the ability of intellectual capital to create wealth was unquestioned when the market valued technology companies with no revenues, no products, and few hard assets in the billions.

Attorneys have certainly recognized this. According to a 2000 survey by the Affiliates, a legal staffing service, nearly half of attorneys polled—48 percent—believe intellectual property will be the hottest practice area in law over the next decade.

One component of intellectual capital is intellectual property. Traditional forms of intellectual property include patents, trademarks, and copyrights. The wide acceptance of the Internet has introduced a fox into the intellectual property henhouse and is driving much of what is happening in intellectual property legislation. Intellectual property issues such as domain name ownership rights, copyrighted materials used as website content, and the patenting of business methods make front-page headlines.

One example of the legislative changes brought about by the Internet was the 1999 passage of the Anti-cybersquatting Consumer Protection Act by Congress. This act prohibits the bad-faith registration, trafficking in, or use of an Internet domain name that is identical to, or confusingly similar to, a distinctive trademark or service mark, or dilutive of a famous trademark or service mark.

Even personal names, protected as trademarks, are subject to the provisions. This was clear in 2000, when Madonna Louise Ciccone laid claim to *www.madonna.com*, a domain name registered to Dan Parisi of Parsippany, New Jersey, who operates a number of adult entertainment sites. Madonna filed a complaint with the World Intellectual Property Organization to reclaim Madonna.com, alleging that Parisi's site represents an "unauthorized, bad faith registration" of her name and trademark. The fight over Madonna.com is the most recent in a string of high-profile domain name disputes. In a similar case, the World Intellectual Property Organization ordered the operator of a parody site about Julia Roberts to surrender Juliaroberts.com to the movie star. But Gordon Sumner, known as Sting, the lead singer of the now-defunct band the Police, lost his bid to win the rights to Sting.com in arbitration, in part because he had not trademarked the name.

The ability of the Internet to reach such a large group of people has radically changed the landscape of intellectual property information. Prior to 1995, much of the information about intellectual properties such as patents and trademarks had been proprietary, controlled by a few specialty information providers.

After the U.S. Government Patent and Trademark Office's website was launched in 1995, patent information became available free of charge through the Internet. Soon patent offices in other countries also begin making their databases available for free on the Internet. Then commercial sites, such as the IBM Intellectual Property Network site (now the Delphion Intellectual Property Network) appeared.

Financial professionals are increasingly finding intellectual property issues in the problems clients are bringing them to solve. Business appraisers may need to identify and value intellectual property in the course of a business valuation. Financial experts are asked to testify in litigation matters involving intellectual property. In this chapter we feature a variety of sites designed to assist the financial profession in understanding, defining, and valuing intellectual property.

All sites are presented in alphabetical order. The sites listed in the "First and Foremost" section of this chapter are those that the authors have found to be reliable, well organized, and rich sources of information. Sites offering all or part of the data for free are considered more desirable than sites offering similar data for a fee. "Best of the Rest" sites may focus on a niche area, be fee only, or have limited navigation and output features.

FIRST AND FOREMOST

Delphion Intellectual Property Network

www.delphion.com   (Exhibit 8.1)

Fee-based site

The Intellectual Property Network began life as an internal IBM project to help researchers, product developers, and intellectual property attorneys perform basic searches of patent data quickly and easily. IBM decided to allow public access to the site, and it become one of the best-known and most widely used patent search sites on the Internet. In 2000 IBM partnered with the Internet Capital Group to set up the Intellectual Property Network as a separate company named Delphion.

The Delphion Intellectual Property Network allows users to search, view, and analyze patent documents. (PDF files containing a patent can be downloaded for $3.00 each.) The depth of the Delphion Intellectual Property Network is impressive. From the Delphion search page at *www.delphion.com/boolquery* you can search the following collections of patent information:

- Complete text and images of all patents issued by the U.S. Patent and Trademark Office since 1974. Bibliographic text descriptions are available for patents between 1971 and 1973. A few patent records prior to 1973 also have images.

- Bibliographic text and full document images from European patent applications from 1979 to present provided by the European Patent Office.

- Bibliographic text and full document images of European patents issued from 1980 to present from the European Patent Office.

- Bibliographic text and representative images of Japanese unexamined patent applications from 1976 (in English) provided by the Japan Patent Information Organization.

- Bibliographic text and representative images from 1990 of World Intellectual Property Organization Patent Cooperation Treaty publications from more than 100 member countries, including the United States. Full document images are available after 1998.

In addition, the Delphion Intellectual Property Network allows searching of the INPADOC (*International Patent Documentation Center*) database, which contains the bibliographic and family data of patent documents and utility models of 65 patent-issuing organizations including the European Patent Office and the World Intellectual Property Organization. Delphion's searchable database makes available 30 million patent family documents and 45 million legal status actions dating from 1968. The site provides the following descriptive information about "patent families" and "legal status actions":

> Patent families represent patents with similar claims from a wide range of countries. This information is useful for identifying the countries in which a patent for a given invention has been applied for or granted. This makes it easier for companies to monitor the import and export strategies of their competitors and to determine the countries in which the invention is not protected and can therefore be freely used. Legal status shows the status, as of a point in time, of a particular patent, as well as members of its patent family, whether it is still valid or has expired. All legal status changes, before and after grant, are listed. Status may officially change before we receive a status update, so you might wish to confirm the status of a given patent with the official government office.

Summaries of IBM *Technical Disclosure Bulletins,* published from 1958 to 1997, are also available for searching and browsing on the Delphion Intellectual Property Network. These bulletins served as forums for IBM employees to publish defensive disclosures of inventions that did not ultimately acquire

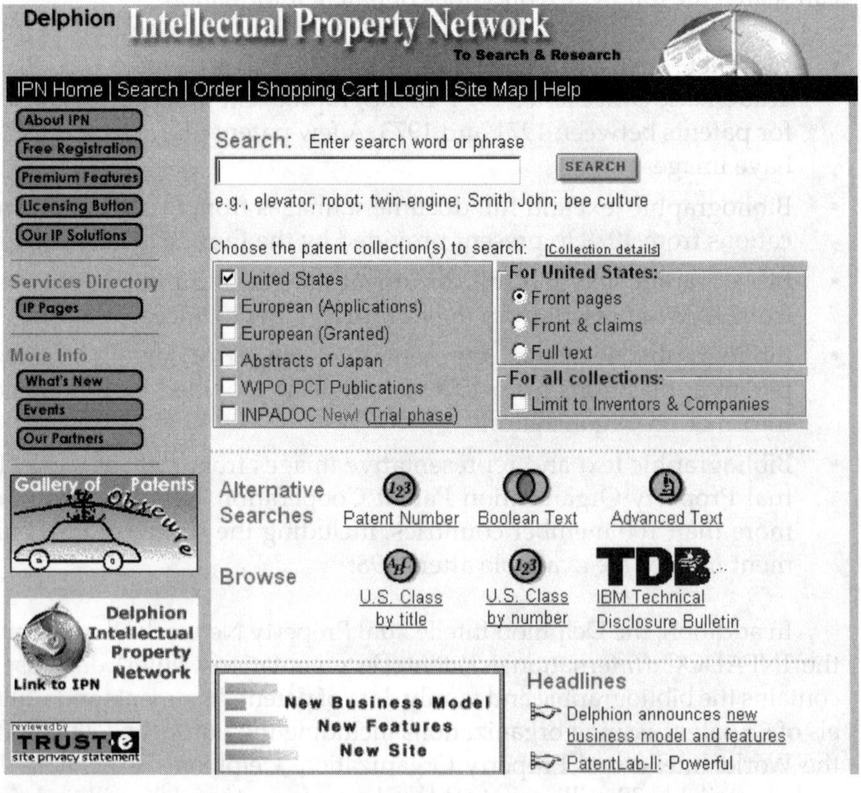

Exhibit 8.1 Delphion Intellectual Property Network
Printed with permission of Delphion, Inc. and the Delphion Intellectual Property Network.

patents. Over the years, these articles became one of the most often cited references in patents. U.S. patents make over 48,000 references to *IBM Technical Disclosure Bulletin* articles.

There are a number of options for searching the databases on Delphion Intellectual Property Network. Searches can be conducted by keyword, patent number, inventor, abstract, or several other categories. Users also can browse categories of patent information. Searching and viewing the patent information is free. In most cases the information can be downloaded for a small fee.

What can you expect to find?

- Detailed information on U.S. patents including full images
- Patent information from Europe and Japan
- Links to other patent resources
- Gallery of unusual patents

The Intellectual Property Mall

www.ipmall.fplc.edu   (Exhibit 8.2)

Fee-based site

The Intellectual Property Mall is a collection of intellectual property resources assembled by the Franklin Pierce Law Center, an American Bar Association–accredited law school located in Concord, New Hampshire. Despite its relatively small size, the Franklin Pierce Law Center is ranked by *U.S. News & World Report* as the third best intellectual property (IP) law school in the nation, trailing only the University of California at Berkeley and George Washington University.

Content is the focus on this site; surprisingly, it is neither particularly slick nor well organized. There is no overall site map or search page, so users must depend on a list of links on the home page and information about content areas on the *www.ipmall.fplc.edu/descriptions.htm* page.

One of the links on the home page will take you to the Franklin Pierce Law Center's IP Library Page. The library considers itself to be the premier intellectual property library in the country. Included in the library's materials are unique collections of practitioner materials donated by intellectual property attorneys and corporate IP departments. The library's user guides, listed on *www.ipmall.fplc.edu/userguid/userguid.htm,* cover the practical ("How to locate IP Periodicals") to the amusing ("Famous U.S. Patents"). Unfortunately, little of the library's extensive collection is accessible through the website.

The Intellectual Property Mall has an extensive listing of intellectual property Web links organized by topic. The index page at *www.ipmall.fplc.edu/pointbox/pointbox.htm* is the best place to start. The collection goes well beyond the obvious well-known links. If you want to find a list of links related to competition law in the European Union or the intellectual property rights of indigenous peoples, this is the place to go.

In the "Tools & Strategies" section of the site you will find briefing papers on a variety of intellectual property topics, ranging from "Trademark Searching: A Desk Reference" to "Determining Date of Invention." The briefing papers tend to be fairly lengthy, with some running 20 to 30 pages; a few, such as "Private Investigators of Intellectual Property," are shorter.

This site makes our "First and Foremost" list because of the interesting content and especially because of the detailed links going to thinly covered niche areas of intellectual property practice. However, it could benefit from a little attention to the many broken links and some effort to update content areas.

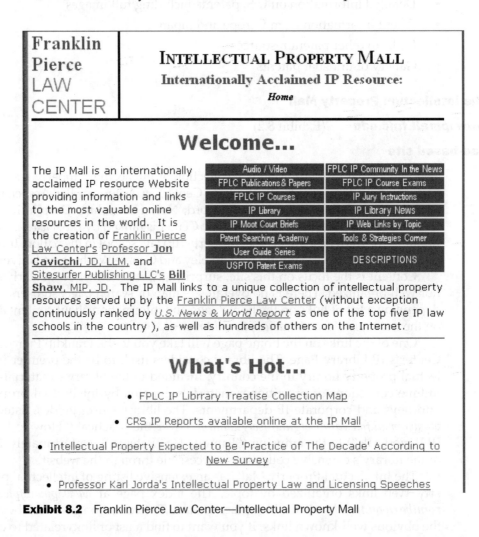

Exhibit 8.2 Franklin Pierce Law Center—Intellectual Property Mall

What can you expect to find?

- Briefing papers on intellectual property topics
- Information about Franklin's top-rated intellectual property library
- Links to a variety of intellectual property sites

The Intellectual Property Transaction Database

www.fvgi.com (Exhibit 8.3)

Fee-based site

The Financial Valuation Group, a business appraisal firm in Tampa, Florida, has developed a proprietary database of empirical research on intellectual property. The searchable database of more than 3,000 transactions is accessible on the Financial Valuation Group's website at *www.fvgi.com.* Information in the Intellectual Property Transaction Database includes data on payments made for royalties and licensing fees for the use of trademarks, patents, copyrights, and brand names.

This compilation of intellectual property transactions was gleaned from publicly available documents, primarily filings with the Securities and Exchange Commission. The transactions pertain to a wide range of industries including:

- Sporting goods
- Software
- Pharmaceuticals
- Apparel
- Medical
- Restaurants
- Telecommunications

The database is searchable either by SIC codes or by the NAICS. A sample of the transaction record showing licensor and licensee information along with the remuneration structure is presented in Exhibit 8.3.

The detailed information on arm's-length transactions in intellectual property is useful to expert witnesses, negotiators, and appraisers. Data from the Intellectual Property Database can be used to support claims for damages in intellectual property litigation cases, estimates of reasonable royalty percentage rates, and valuations of closely held companies and other intangible assets.

Example of Transaction Data Available - Summary of Licensing Agreement

Licensor: Name of Company/Person who receives the royalty	Cornell Research Foundation, Inc.	**Licensee:** Name of Company/Person who pays the royalty	International Canine Genetics, Inc.
Licensor 1987 SIC: 4-digit SIC number	8733	**Licensee 1987 SIC:** 4-digit SIC number	2834
Licensor 1997 NAICS: 6-digit NAICS number	541710	**Licensee 1997 NAICS:** 6-digit NAICS number	325412
Licensor Country: Country	U.S.	**Licensee Country:** Country	U.S.
Licensor Industry: Brief description of industry of licensor in relation to SIC/NAICS numbers	Research Foundation	**Licensee Industry:** Brief description of industry of licensee in relation to SIC/NAICS numbers	Pharmaceutical Preparations
Type of Agreement: Type of intellectual property being licensed (i.e., patent, trademark, etc.)	Patent	**Term of Agreement:** Period of time license agreement is in effect, if applicable (years only)	
Secondary Type: Secondary field for type of property being licensed (when applicable)	Technology	**Term Type:** Perpetual, patent life, years, etc.	Patent Life
Patent or Trademark Number: Government assigned patent or trademark registration number, if applicable		**Month of LA:** Month of actual agreement	11
		Day of LA: Day of actual agreement	6
		Year: Year of actual agreement	1995
Geographic Region: Geographic area where the rights are being granted (i.e., US, Worldwide, Europe, etc.)	U.S.	**Original or Amended:** Original unless source document indicates this is an amendment to earlier agreement	Original
General Industry: Overall industry of the transaction	Veterinary Pharmaceuticals	**Description of Product or Service:** Brief synopsis of the transaction	Patent for dog pregnancy testing
Remuneration Structure: Describes how the royalties are paid (i.e. percent of revenues, flat fee, per unit, annual fee,	Flat Fee/Percent		
Flat %: Flat royalty percentage rate (if applicable)	6.00%	**Flat Fee:** Flat royalty amount in dollars (if applicable)	$50,000.00
Range % Low End: Percentage with low-end sliding scale (if applicable)		**Range $ Low End:** Low-end sliding scale in dollars (if applicable)	
Range % High End: Percentage with high-end sliding scale (if applicable)		**Range $ High End:** High-end sliding scale in dollars (if applicable)	
Percent Based On: Brief definition of basis for payment of percentage royalties (i.e. net sales, gross sales, etc.)	Net sales price	**Dollar Royalty Based On:** Brief definition of basis for payment of dollar royalties (i.e. annual fee, per unit sold, flat fee, etc.)	Up front fee plus 6% of net sales price
Base Definition: Further defines the basis of fee or royalty, if necessary, such as figure to define a sliding scale	$25,000 Up front license fee	**Comments:** Other pertinent information	
Guaranteed Annual Royalty: Minimum dollar royalty paid annually independent of actual net sales, gross sales, etc.	$10,000	**Source Document:** Original document type where data was retrieved (i.e., 10-Q, an excerpt of 10-K verbiage, etc.)	License Agreement
Maximum Fee for Life of Agreement: Financial dollar cap after which no further royalties are due		**Date of Source Document:** Date of the source document	11/06/1995
		ID #: FVG control #	760

Exhibit 8.3 Example of Transaction Data Available—Summary of Licensing Agreement

What can you expect to find?

- Royalty rate percentages paid in actual transactions
- Over 35 fields of data on each intellectual property transaction

Law.com Intellectual Law Practice Center

www.law.com/professionals/iplaw.html   (Exhibit 8.4)

Fee-based site

Law.com is a commercial site targeting attorneys and law students. The umbrella site, *www.law.com,* is divided into five practice areas. In addition to the IP Center, there are practice areas for Corporate Law, Employment Law, Litigation, and Tech Law.

All of the practice areas strive to offer one-stop shopping for the busy practitioner with coverage of breaking legal news, the latest case law, and practical information and legal analysis. The IP Center focuses on legal developments in the areas of patents, trademarks, copyrights, trade secrets, and unfair competition. Biotechnology, media, and entertainment law issues receive a lot of attention.

The IP News is well designed and content rich. The full text of current articles from publications such as the *American Lawyer* and the *National Law Journal* are displayed along with pictures, illustrations, and links to related articles. The IP News section also picks up intellectual property stories from daily and weekly legal newspapers in Washington, D.C., New York, California, Texas, Pennsylvania, Florida, New Jersey, and Connecticut.

The Decisions and Authority section offers a summary of recent case decisions from all the federal circuits, the United States Supreme Court, and the appellate courts of most states. Detailed case analyses and the full citations of cases are available to subscribers who pay a small annual fee.

The site also features the full text of intellectual property articles from other publications, such as *The Industry Standard,* and practice tools, such as sample agreements and other legal documents. Practice papers are available to subscribers; they offer original, authoritative analysis by experienced practitioners and recognized experts on hot intellectual property topics. Recent practice papers have included "Copyright Law: Fair Use and the Internet" and "The Changing Face of Patent Practice."

What can you expect to find?

- Articles from law journals on intellectual property topics
- Cases on intellectual property issues
- Practice papers that cover a topic in depth

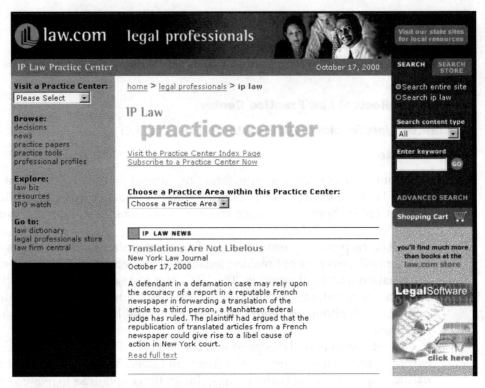

Exhibit 8.4   Law.com—IP Law Practice Center

- A law dictionary and links to state legal resources
- An online store where you can purchase books and software

Patent Café

www.patentcafe.com   (Exhibit 8.5)

Free and Fee-based site

Patent Café has positioned itself as a resource for inventors. Its founder describes it as "a portal for patent, trademark, and copyright information, advice, and community networking."

There is a lot of data here. In fact, Patent Café is actually composed of a number of separate properties with unique URLs under common ownership. These sister sites include Patent Café Magazine (*www.cafezine.com*); Lock My Doc (*www.lockmydoc.com*), a digital document file management portal; Patent Café Mall (*www.ipbookstore.com*), an intellectual property bookstore; and Patent Café Community (*www.cafeforums.com*).

If you are looking for basic intellectual property information, start your visit to Patent Café at the Frequently Asked Questions (FAQ) page *www. patentcafe.com/faq.* Here you will find dozens of questions and answers on intellectual property topics. There are FAQ sections on patents, trade markets, international patents, trade secrets, copyrights, and patent applications. The FAQ answers are well done. If an answer refers to another document, such as the Trade Secret Act, the FAQ answer provides a link to the referred document. There is even a listing at *www.patentcafe.com/patents_etc_cafe/morfaq.html* of intellectual property FAQs on other sites, such as the United States Patent Office site.

The PatentCafe.com magazine publishes each month new articles by business and invention experts. The topics covered lean to the practical, such as "How to Market Your Patent," "Invention Feasibility Checklist," and "Submitting Your Invention to Industry." But there are articles on more sophisticated issues, such as information on the revision of European patent conventions and a discussion on the Uniform Information Transaction Act.

You can search for articles appearing in the Patent Café magazine from the search page at *www.cafezine.com/search_data.asp?deptId=15.* Articles are also organized under topic headings (News and Opinions, Invention and Innovation, Technology Enterprise, Intellectual Property Law, Kids Discovery, Tech Transfer/Licensing, and WorldView International). Clicking on one of these links will take you to a selection of articles in that topic area. Users can personalize the content by setting up a personal folder called My Magazine that allows them to save articles, book reviews, or news features.

Exhibit 8.5 PatentCafe.com
Printed by permission, Copyright 1996–2000, PatentCafe.com, Inc.

From the home page you can link to collections of resources by area of interest. Clicking on the small businesses resource page will take you to dozens of links, articles, and forms directed at small business needs. There are similar interest areas for attorneys, teachers, and inventors.

The Patent Café makes an effort to address a concern common to most sites targeting inventors: fraud. An entire section on the site is devoted to fraud issues; see *www.patentcafe.com/inventors_cafe/fraud.html.* Here inventors can learn how to avoid scams and report fraudulent activities.

The Patent Café Mall sells books, software, and documents through partners such as Amazon.com and Marketresearch.com. In addition to these expected items, you also can purchase posters of historical patent drawings. (The drawing of the original Porsche 911 is a favorite.) If you fall in love with the site, you can also get an official Patent Café hat or mouse pad here.

In the fall of 2000, a new intellectual property site was added to the Patent Café family. The IP Search Engine site at *www.IPSearchEngine.com* allows users to search from a single page a number of intellectual property databases worldwide. The site overlays a search page over databases from patent issuing entities such as the U.S. Patent Office and the European Patent Office.

Some users may take issue with the overt commercialism of the Patent Café site. Ads permeate the site, and some links are misleading. Headings that appear to be instructive—for example, "How to Protect Your Idea"—take you to ads for Patent Café partners.

What can you expect to find?

- Lots of how-tos for inventors, how to patent/sell/market/exploit your invention
- Articles on a variety of intellectual property issues
- Links to commercial intellectual property service providers
- A patent exchange listing service
- Chat rooms and discussion lists for inventors
- Bookstore of intellectual property resources

The United States Copyright Office

http://lcweb.loc.gov/copyright   (Exhibit 8.6)

Free site

The website for the United States Copyright Office is part of the Library of Congress site. This should be your first stop for copyright data. The copyright basics page at *www.loc.gov/copyright/circs/circ1.html* provides detailed information on the practical aspects of copyright use and law.

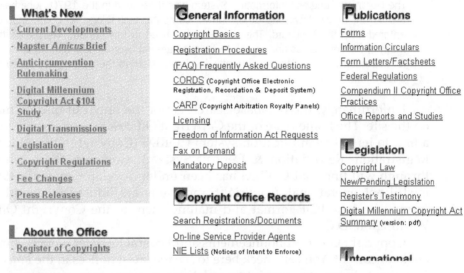

Exhibit 8.6 United States Copyright Office: The Library of Congress

The Copyright Basic page is part of the "Copyright Information Circulars and Form Letters" section that forms the core of the site. Here you can download dozens of fact sheets, letters, and opinions covering a wide variety of copyright issues, from "Copyright Registration for Online Work" to "Reproductions of Copyrighted Works by Educators and Librarians."

Library of Congress Information System makes available U.S. Copyright Office records, including registration information and recorded documents. There are three searchable databases:

- The COHM database, which is updated weekly, covers records for materials registered for copyright since January 1978. Included are books, films, music, maps, sound recordings, software, multimedia kits, drawings, posters, sculpture, and so on.

- The COHS database is updated semiannually and covers periodicals, magazines, journals, newspapers, and other serials registered for copyright since 1978.

- The COHD database, updated weekly, covers references to documents relating to copyright ownership legal transactions, such as name changes and transfers.

The good news is that these databases are open to public searching; the bad news is that users are forced to search using an antiquated telnet text-based system. The Copyright Office acknowledges that this may be a problem for some users by including the following disclaimer on its search page:

> The Library of Congress Information System was developed in the 1970s long before the advent of Windows and other current computer technology. All commands are entered from the keyboard. The mouse is not used in this system. We realize that many of the commands and search techniques are not user-friendly, and we apologize for this inconvenience. We are currently developing state-of-the-art software to replace this system.

Unfortunately, the database search is not the only out-of-date material on the site. The home page of the Copyright Office site prominently features a link to its online application system CORDS (Copyright Office Electronic Registration, Recordation & Deposit System). However, those who click through will find that CORDS has been under development since 1993 but is still not operational. Copyright applicants are limited to downloading forms in Adobe PDF format and mailing them to the Copyright Office in Washington, D.C.

Copyright Office Announcements and Federal Register Notices, however, are kept current. You can check here to see the latest notices in the *Federal Register* about changes in copyright regulations.

What can you expect to find?

- Frequently asked questions about copyright issues
- Searchable database of copyrights
- Summary of copyright legislation

The United States Patent and Trademark Office

www.uspto.gov   (Exhibit 8.7)

Free site

The United States Patent and Trademark Office (PTO) is ground zero for intellectual property rights in the United States. The primary services provided by PTO include processing patents and trademarks and disseminating patent and trademark information. In 1999 the PTO's 6,000 employees processed more

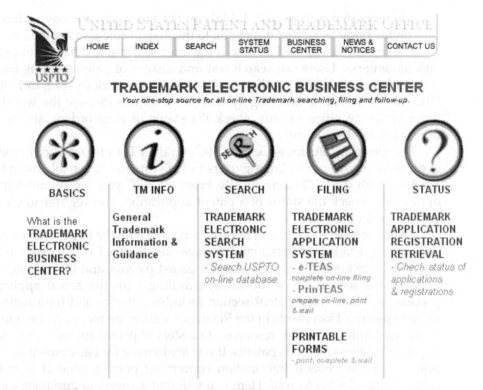

Exhibit 8.7 U.S. Patent and Trademark Office

than 272,000 patent and 297,000 trademark applications and granted 145,000 and 88,000, respectively.

In October 2000 PTO introduced an electronic patent filing system. Software that applicants can use to compose and file the patent application is free on the PTO site. The PTO has accepted trademark applications electronically since October 1998.

The amount of information on the PTO site is daunting, and navigating the site can be a chore. The site index at *www.uspto.gov/web/navaids/siteindx.htm* is a 14-page alphabetized listing of website sections that can be more confusing than helpful. For example, under the "D" section, there is a "Drawing" link and a "Drawing Page" link. With no explanation and no context to draw on, site visitors must visit the pages to discover that the "Drawing" page lists the standards to which a patent drawing must adhere and the "Drawing Page" defines what the application page containing a trademark presentation must look like.

There is an attempt to help steer users to the more popular pages. A button at the top right of the home page carries an invitation to "visit our most frequently requested web pages." I'd take my chances with the navigation buttons on the home page that direct you to the major topic areas of the site.

The centerpiece of the PTO site is the huge searchable database of patents and trademarks. Users can search text and images of patents dating back to 1976 and registered and pending trademarks dating back to 1870. In 1999 the PTO added an online ordering system so customers can use the website to order copies of office records, check the status of their orders, and receive patent copies electronically.

The Electronic Business Center (EBC) on the PTO site (*www.uspto.gov/ebc*) is the e-commerce portal linking users to the systems that enable them to do business with the PTO electronically. From the EBC you can submit a patent application, check the status of a patent application, and register to conduct business with the PTO.

If you are looking for patent information, start with the Patent home page at *www.uspto.gov/web/menu/pats.html*. This page classifies the PTO's patent information into three areas: (1) applications, (2) issued patents, and (3) reference. The Applications section covers documents dealing with the actual application process, and the Issued Patent section includes statistics and information on existing patents. Documents in the Reference section are more diverse, ranging from independent inventor resources, to rosters of patent attorneys, to a white paper on business methods patents. If you are looking for basic patent information, go to the General Information concerning patents page at *www.uspto .gov/web/offices/pac/doc/general*. Here you will find answers to questions such as "What can be patented?" and "Who may apply for a patent?"

Similarly, the Trademark home page at *www.uspto.gov/web/menu/tm.html* gives access to trademark resources such as the U.S. Trademark Electronic Search System (TESS), online trademark applications, and legal resources, such as guidelines for the trademark registration of Internet domain names. The Trademark Electronic Business Center section of the site at *www.uspto. gov/web/menu/tmebc/index.html* is the PTO's attempt to provide a single place to locate all the different electronic search systems and methods of doing trademark business. From here you can access the TESS search system, file a trademark application, or check on the status of existing applications.

The PTO Information Dissemination Service has created an online products and services catalog at *www.uspto.gov/web/offices/ac/ido/oeip/catalog/index.html*. The products include such items as a print version of the "Code of Federal Regulations, Title 37 Patents, Trademarks, and Copyrights" and a video on how to conduct a patent search.

If you are interested in the DNA patents issued by the PTO, see the DNA Patent Database at *http://208.201.146.119*. The Foundation for Genetic Medicine and the Georgetown University Kennedy Institute of Ethics have joined together to offer the full-text of DNA patents at this site.

What can you expect to find?

- Trademarks and patents definitions and basic information
- Searchable database of patents and trademarks
- Full text of the *PTO Magazine,* a 30- to 40-page color publication covering current intellectual property issues at the PTO
- U.S. Trademark law rules of practice and federal statutes
- Online applications for patents and trademarks
- The *Commissioner of Patents and Trademarks Annual Reports,* containing detailed statistical information on intellectual property

University of Texas Copyright Crash Course

www.utsystem.edu/OGC/IntellectualProperty/cprtindx.htm   (Exhibit 8.8)

Free site

The Copyright Crash Course developed by attorneys in the office of the University of Texas General Council is copyright education by the immersion method. This is an excellent introductory resource to copyright law for the layperson. The site was designed for faculty and students at the University of Texas who are using copyrighted materials in the development of new courses, as supplemental materials, and as part of student projects. Some of the materials will be of interest only to those in academia (i.e., the excellent discussion paper entitled "Ownership of Lectures—Commercial Notetaking in University Courses"). But most of the information has a much broader appeal.

The Fair Use section of the site is an 18-page discourse that includes a section on individual liability for infringement, a walkthrough of the four-factor fair use test, and rules of thumb for fair use of various types of copyrighted materials. There is also a detailed analysis of the way that the Texaco case changed the concept of fair use. (In this case the court found that Texaco's practice of copying of journal articles by or for its scientists was an infringement of the copyright owners' exclusive rights.) If the material cannot be used under the fair use exception, users are directed to the "Getting Permission" section of the site, which covers in detail how to identify copyright owners and obtain permissions to use copyrighted works.

Georgia Harper, the attorney primarily responsible for this site, has contributed a number of interesting monographs on various copyright issues. These include "University Copy Centers: Do They Pass the Fair Use Test?" "Will We Need Fair Use in the Twenty-First Century?" "Limitations on the Performance Right: Video, Audio, and Radio," and "Professionals' Fair Use of Journal Articles for Scholarship, Reference and Research."

Sections on the site cover the rule for using materials available on the Internet. More than two dozen presentations (some in PowerPoint format and some in HTML) covering various copyright issues are available for viewing on the site.

A tutorial on the site takes visitors through a series of scenarios about copyright use and then tests them on their knowledge.

What you can expect to find?

- Insightful commentary on copyright issues by the general counsel of the University of Texas
- Copyright basics with links to the underlying legislation
- Guidelines for acquiring copyright permissions
- Presentations on a variety of copyright-related topics

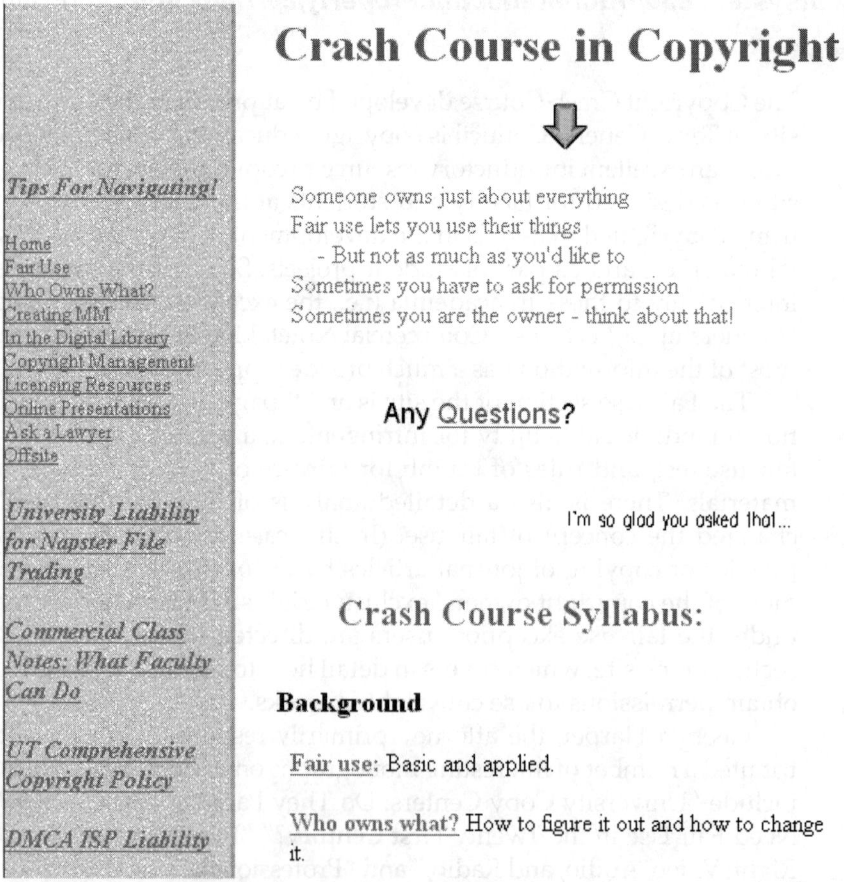

Crash Course in Copyright

Tips For Navigating!

Home
Fair Use
Who Owns What?
Creating MM
In the Digital Library
Copyright Management
Licensing Resources
Online Presentations
Ask a Lawyer
Offsite

University Liability for Napster File Trading

Commercial Class Notes: What Faculty Can Do

UT Comprehensive Copyright Policy

DMCA ISP Liability

Someone owns just about everything
Fair use lets you use their things
   - But not as much as you'd like to
Sometimes you have to ask for permission
Sometimes you are the owner - think about that!

Any Questions?

I'm so glad you asked that...

Crash Course Syllabus:

Background

Fair use: Basic and applied.

Who owns what? How to figure it out and how to change it.

Exhibit 8.8 Crash Course in Copyright
Georgia Harper, University of Texas System.

World Intellectual Property Organization

www.wipo.org

Free site

The World Intellectual Property Organization (WIPO) is an international organization dedicated to helping ensure that the rights of creators and owners of intellectual property are protected worldwide. The WIPO operates as a specialized agency of the United Nations. Currently 175 counties, including the United States, are WIPO members. WIPO has assumed a leading role in drafting agreements and legislation dealing with intellectual property issues related to the Internet. The WIPO site includes copies of treaties, statistical information, and articles on the latest developments in this focus area.

The WIPO site is divided into four sections:

1. About WIPO
2. About Intellectual Property
3. News and Information Resources
4. Activities and Services

In the first section you will find background on the WIPO including full-color 40-plus-page annual reports dating from 1997. There is also information on the 21 treaties administered by the WIPO in the field of intellectual property. These treaties cover internationally agreed on standards of intellectual property protection in each country, registrations and filings, and classification systems.

The About Intellectual Property section contains a brief general discussion about patents, trademarks, and copyrights. This section also contains a discussion on a topic unique to the WIPO site: "geographical indications." Geographical indications refers to the use of place names to add value to the product or service associated with them. The WIPO site lists the following examples: "Champagne," "Cognac," "Roquefort," "Chianti," "Pilsen," "Porto," "Sheffield," "Havana," "Tequila," and "Darjeeling." (Apparently the WIPO does not recognize any geographical indications within the United States.)

The News and Information Resources section provides the "meat" of the useful information on the site. Here you will find downloadable copies of the WIPO magazine in Adobe PDF format. Recent issues have included articles such as "New Issues in Domain Name Abuse," "Resolving Cybersquatting Disputes," and "Modernization of Intellectual Property Systems in Least Developed Countries." The WIPO Electronic Bookshop is also on this page offering dozens of publications for purchase.

This section also contains a link to the various intellectual property data collections currently hosted by the WIPO at *http://ipdl.wipo.int.* Here you will find 15 searchable databases housing patent and trademark information from various countries. Also in this section is the Collection of Laws for Electronic Access (CLEA) database, an electronic archive of intellectual property legislation. CLEA contains the full text of intellectual property legislation of a number of countries and the European Community as well as the full text of all treaties administered by WIPO.

The fourth section of the site, Activities and Services, covers the programs administered by the WIPO. These include a Distance Learning Program, a Professional Training Program, a Policy Training Program, Joint Diploma Courses, and the Library.

If you are looking for patent and trademark information for Canada or Europe, try the Canadian Intellectual Property Office at *http://strategis.ic.gc.ca/sc_mrksv/cipo* and the European Patent Office at *www.epo.co.at.*

What can you expect to find?

- Databases of patent information for the United States, Europe, Asia, Latin America, and India
- Downloadable documents, such as the "Guide to the International Registration of Marks"
- Articles from the WIPO magazine and other WIPO publications
- Text of intellectual property treaties from around the world
- Online courses on intellectual property basics

BEST OF THE REST

ABA Intellectual Property Law Section

www.abanet.org/intelprop

Free site

The Intellectual Property Law section (formerly the Section of Patent, Trademark and Copyright Law) of the American Bar Association (ABA) is the largest intellectual property organization in the United States. Membership in the section is limited to members of the bar association, but the section's website has a number of resources available to the public.

For those interested in developments in intellectual property law, the section tracks relevant legislation and reports the status on current bills in Congress. The publications section allows visitors to purchase some basic intellectual property booklets. However, to purchase the section's primary product, "The Patent Litigation Strategies Handbook," visitors are directed to the Bureau of National Affairs (BNA) book site at *www.bnabooks.com/publications/details/d_plst.htm.*

Association of Research Libraries Copyright and IP Center

http://arl.cni.org/info/frn/copy/copytoc.html

Free site

No one is surprised that libraries have a great interest in copyright developments and trends. The Association of Research Libraries (ARL) has put together a collection of copyright resources as part of its Federal Relations and Information Policy Program.

The site has information on current legislation including congressional testimony on various pieces of copyright legislation. You also will find information on international developments in copyright law. During the fall of 2000, when the music-trading site Napster was on trial, the ARL site posted information related to the case including amicus briefs. As the ARL is involved in lobbying activities, the legislation coverage is slanted toward the issues of most interest to ARL members, as are the articles covering copyright issues from the ARL newsletter available on the site at *http://arl.cni.org/newsltr/copy.html.*

One of the most interesting features on the site is a historical timeline that traces the development of copyright law since its enactment into U.S. federal law in 1790 at *http://arl.cni.org/info/frn/copy/timeline.html.* The timeline includes coverage of landmark cases, statutory amendments, and international conventions, many of which contain hyperlinks to the applicable text.

BitLaw

www.bitlaw.com

Free site

Daniel A. Tysver, a partner with the Minnesota-based intellectual property law firm of Beck & Tysver, created BitLaw as an Internet resource on technology law. The BitLaw site contains more than 1,800 pages on patent, copyright, trademark, and Internet legal issues.

BitLaw is a well-designed site brimming with original content. Tysver has done an excellent job of presenting well-written primers on patents, trademarks, and copyrights. Be sure to check out the Software Patent Index page at *www.bitlaw.com/software-patent/index.html.* The BitLaw Introduction to Software Patents not only covers the basics on this topic but also includes an interesting discourse on bad software patents. BitLaw also links to a selection of articles on software patents, including a very interesting discussion on the software patent process from *Wired* magazine. (See "Patently Absurd" at *www.wired.com/wired/archive/2.07/patents.html.*)

The Internet Law section of BitLaw covers topics such as Web Site Development, Legal Issues, Service Provider Liability, Trademarks on the Internet,

Domain Name Disputes, and Web Page Linking and Legal Liability. The site's weak areas include the "primary sources" section and the "legal links" section. As of the date of this writing, these two sections contained a number of broken and out-of-date links and the articles were not current.

Consor

www.consor.com

Fee-based site

Consor is a "market-based consulting firm specializing in intellectual property valuations, royalty rates and all areas of licensing." In addition to consulting services, Consor provides market-based data on royalty rates, values, and licensing customs and practices. Consor characterizes this as "the largest proprietary index of licensing and valuation data encompassing over 8,000 transactions." Unfortunately, at publication time this proprietary index was not accessible on the Consor website, so users must call or e-mail Consor to purchase the information.

Copyright Clearance Center

www.copyright.com

Fee-based site

The Copyright Clearance Center (CCC) is a nonprofit licensing agent for text reproduction rights. The center facilitates compliance with U.S. copyright law by "licensing systems for the reproduction and distribution of copyrighted materials in print and electronic formats."

The CCC manages rights for more than 9,600 publishers and hundreds of thousands of authors. Users of CCC include corporations, government agencies, trade associations, law firms, document suppliers, libraries, academic institutions, copy shops, and bookstores.

On this site, the CCC hosts an extensive database of permissions for purchase. Want to make copies of an article from the *Business Valuation Review*? Click on the database search button and search by title to find it and purchase the right to copy. Note that the database contains only citations for the materials, not the full text.

CorporateIntelligence

http://corporateintelligence.com

Free and Fee-based site

CorporateIntelligence.com is the parent site for several well-known intellectual property companies, including MicroPatent, Faxpat, Optipat, 1790.com, and Master Data Center. CorporateIntelligence.com uses these companies to provide services for researching, managing, and licensing patents, trademarks, and other types of intellectual property on a global basis. In 2000 CorporateIntelligence.com added the trademark.com site to its brood of sites for searching databases on federal, state, and common law.

On the CorporateIntelligence.com site home page you will find current news stories about intellectual property issues and a special "Issues and Answers" section, one of the best sections of the site. Here you will find attorneys, professors, and industry experts like Frank Landgraff, patent and technology counsel for The Coca-Cola Company, Scott M. Alter, partner with Hale and Dorr LLP, and Paul Lerner, general counsel of General Patent Corporation, writing in-depth articles on a variety of IP topics. Recent articles have included "Strategic Auditing: The Key to Minimizing Litigation Bills," "Measuring and Managing Value Creation," "Ruling on Damages Could Turn Patent Holders into Paper Tigers," and "Officer and Director Liability for Mismanagement of Intellectual Property."

The site also has what it claims to be "the only available Patent and Trademark litigation database on the Internet." The rest of the information on the site is provided by links to CorporateIntelligence's other companies (listed below), some of which offer competing products and charge a fee for their services.

- MicroPatent (*www.micropat.com*). Search the more than 33 million digital patents from the United States, Europe, Asia, and Africa.
- Master Data Center (*www.masdata.com*). Provides patent and trademark annuity payment services.
- Faxpat (*www.faxpat.com/index.html*). Provides copies of issued patents and trademarks by fax. Also offers patent and trademark file histories.
- Optipat (*www.optipat.com*). Provides copies of patents on CD-ROM and other patent and trademark document services, such as file histories. It is being assimilated by MicroPatent.
- 1790.com (*www.1790.com*). Access to full-text U.S. patent research with specialized software for repackaging patent data for corporate distribution.
- Trademark.com (*www.trademark.com*). Searchable database of federal, state, and common-law trademarks.

Department of Energy Patent Databases

www.osti.gov/waisgate/gchome2.html

Free site

At this site users can search patents and patent applications owned by the Department of Energy (DOE) or its contractors. There is a cumulative database that includes DOE patents that were developed since 1978 and patent applications processed for the Energy Science and Technology Database (EDB) after January 1993. The Current Release Database contains recent EDB patents and patent applications. Most of the data is presented in the form of a bibliographic citation but some patents in the Current Release database are full-text.

Intellectual Property Law Web Server

www.patents.com

Free site

The Colorado law firm of Oppedahl & Larson maintains the Intellectual Property Law Web Server, a collection of information on copyright, patents, trademark, trade secrets, and computer law. The site is painfully plain, devoid of any graphics, site maps, or search tools. But one advantage of such a stripped-down site is that it is viewable in even the most ancient browser.

The site is filled with original content. The patent page at *www.patents.com/patents.htm* contains 38 pages of patent information ranging from an explanation of the International Patent Cooperation Treaty to the definition of patent prosecution. The copyright page at *www.patents.com/copyrigh.htm* and the trademark page at *www.patents.com/trademar.htm* contain similar treasure troves of information on those topics.

The "Web Law" page at *www.patents.com/weblaw.htm* also contains excellent original content but suffers from the site's sporadic updating. Some parts of this page were recently updated as of this writing, but others have not been freshened since the site was launched in 1996.

If the Intellectual Property Law Web Server site were updated and redesigned, we could consider it a "First and Foremost" site. Still, the great, if dated, original content makes it a "Best of the Rest" site.

Intellectual Property Owners Association

www.ipo.org

Fee-based site

The Intellectual Property Owners (IPO) Association focuses exclusively on protecting rights of intellectual property owners. The site shines with its news service and legislative and judicial updates. The IPO Daily News announces intellectual property developments, including court cases, current legislation, and alerts to intellectual property stories in the news. The "IP in the Courts" section summarizes precedential opinions of the U.S. Court of Appeals for the Federal Circuit. The IPO site also maintains an annual list of the top patent holders based on filings with the U.S. Patent & Trademark Office.

International Trademark Association

www.inta.org

Fee-based site

The International Trademark Association, a group of more than 3,700 members in 121 countries, works to promote trademarks in international commerce. The association's website includes information on a variety of topics, including Brand Valuation, Trademark Licensing, Trademark Infringements and Statutory Redress, and European Community Trademarks. You also can purchase intellectual property books and resources published by the International Trademark Association.

Journal of Technology Law & Policy

http://dogwood.circa.ufl.edu/~techlaw

Free site

The *Journal of Technology Law & Policy* is a project of the University of Florida College of Law to publish articles that focus on the legal and policy aspects of various technology issues. The site has the full text of articles on a number of intellectual property issues. Recent articles in the *Journal of Technology Law & Policy* have focused on Internet copyright violations ("The Case of the Invisible Infringer: Trademarks, Metatags and Initial Interest Confusion" and "Trademarks, Internet Domain Names, and the NSI: How Do We Fix a System That Is Already Broken?")

A number of law schools have similar journals that analyze in detail IP issues, especially as they apply to technology. The *Marquette Intellectual Property Law Review* (*www.marquette.edu/law/ipwebpage/iplawrev.html*) and the *Jour-*

nal of Intellectual Property Law at the University of Georgia (*www.lawsch. uga.edu/~jipl/index.html*) are examples of other student-edited journals. A list of technology and intellectual property journals from other universities can be found at *http://palm.circa.ufl.edu/~techlaw/links*.

Kuester Law Technology Law Resource

www.kuesterlaw.com

Free site

Jeffrey Kuester, a patent, copyright, and trademark attorney with the Atlanta firm of Thomas, Kayden, Horstemeyer & Risley, maintains the Kuester Law Technology Law Resource site. This site has garnered attention for its detailed list of links to intellectual property resources. Unfortunately, there is little original content here beyond the short articles in the Basic Info section that discuss the rudiments of patents and trademarks. To read some of the excellent articles on IP issues authored by Kuester and the other attorneys at his firm, go to the articles page on the Thomas, Kayden, Horstemeyer & Risley site (*www.tkhr.com/articles.html*).

Lexis-Nexis Intellectual Property Solution

www.lexis.com

Fee-based site

Lexis has a comprehensive patent database that includes the full text of patents since 1971 along with more than 18 million images and drawings. Lexis adds a notation to the text record of the patent that includes all the changes that occur during the life of the patent including ownership changes and litigation status. There is also a wealth of trademark information and intellectual property regulations. The site is limited to subscribers only. Subscription prices vary based on products accessed and firm size but can run several thousand dollars annually.

Musicians' Intellectual Law & Resources

www.aracnet.com/~schornj/index.shtml

Free site

Copyright issues in the music industry have been in the headlines in recent years. Stories about the Napster case and international sales of illegal CDs has focused attention on the role of copyrights in the protection of composers' and musicians' rights. Attorney Jay M. Schornstein created this site, which focuses on copyright law as it applies to music, largely in response to the horror stories he witnessed in the music business and to the requests from his music and entertainment clients for references to intellectual law information.

The Musicians' Intellectual Law & Resources site has information on copyrighting compositions and sound recordings; collection of royalties; and locating and working with booking agents, managers, and music publishers. It also discusses record contracts and compares recording contract clauses with samples of contracts and other legal documents. As a reward for slogging through all the legal and legislative information, Schornstein lists his favorite jazz and blues websites.

If you are interested in more information about copyright as it relates to the music industry, Recording Industry Association of America's (RIAA) Web page at *www.riaa.com* has a good overview of musical copyright issues as well as licensing and royalties. RIAA has set up a separate site at *www.soundbyting.com/html/index.html* to inform the public about the problems of copyright abuse in the music industry and address some misconceptions about downloading information from the Internet.

Stanford Copyright and Fair Use

http://fairuse.stanford.edu

Free site

This site, hosted by Stanford University, addresses the doctrine of fair use, which permits limited use of copyrighted materials by persons who are not the copyright holders. Fair use is a contentious and confusing element of copyright law, and the Stanford University Library system has compiled a collection of resources to address this issue. A good explanation of the fair use concept can be found by clicking on the first link at the top of the home page, which leads to a memorandum written by Stanford provost Condoleezza Rice at *http://fairuse.stanford.edu/rice.html*. According to Rice, the memorandum "provides a general description of the applicability of the copyright law and the so-called 'fair use' exemptions to the copyright law's general prohibition on copying. It also describes 'safe harbor' guidelines applicable to classroom copying."

The remainder of the site contains links to related statutes, resources, and articles. While home to a core of good information on the fair use concept, at the date of this writing the site was suffering from a lack of attention. Many links are bad and most of the articles and legislative information appear to come from the years 1996 to 1998.

Those interested in the concept of fair use may also want to visit the Fair Use Guidelines for Educational Multimedia and Related Documents site at Penn State (*www.libraries.psu.edu/mtss/fairuse/default.html*).

The Trade Secrets Homepage

www.rmarkhalligan.com/index2.html

Free site

Mark Halligan, a Chicago attorney, has created a website devoted to a frequently overlooked type of intellectual property, trade secrets. Halligan is a trial lawyer who gained extensive jury trial experience litigating trade secret, patent, copyright, and trademark cases and related antitrust, unfair competition, and licensing issues around the country. His site covers various aspects of trade secret law, including trade secret audits, licensing, and third-party liability for misappropriation. There is an archive of cases dealing specifically with trade secrets and the text of related legislation such as the Uniform Trade Secrets Act.

U.S. Patent Citation Database—Community of Science

http://patents.cos.com

Fee-based site

The U.S. Patents database is a searchable bibliographic file containing approximately 2.6 million U.S. patents issued since 1975. The database includes basic information about each patent: number, dates, assignee, inventor, title, abstract, exemplary claims for recent years, and U.S. and international classifications. Also included in each record is the lineage of each patent—how each patent cites previous patents or is cited by subsequent ones. Access is limited to subscribers. Individual subscription run $250 annually.

The WATCH File at the University of Texas

www.hrc.utexas.edu/watch/watch.html

Free site

If you are only going to do one thing, do it well. The WATCH File (writers, artists, and their copyright holders) has a very specific mission, which it accomplishes admirably.

The WATCH File is a database containing the names and addresses of copyright holders. There is also information for archivists of authors' and artists' collections that are housed in libraries in North America and in the United Kingdom. WATCH is a joint project of the Harry Ransom Humanities Research Center at the University of Texas at Austin and the University of Reading Library, Reading, England.

The WATCH File was established to provide scholars with information about whom to contact for permission to publish text and images under copyright, but it can be useful to anyone who seeks to use copyrighted material. The site contains an excellent discourse on "Locating Copyright Holders" at *www.hrc.utexas.edu/watch/locating.html*. The searchable database of copyright holders is accessible at *http://hemingway.hrc.utexas.edu/watchfiles/WATCHMenu. htm*.

Tax and Accounting

Eva M. Lang

Accountants have been late adopters when it comes to computer technologies. Accounting firms were among the last groups of users to abandon DOS. Perhaps abandon is not the right word; according to a 2000 survey of accountants, 3 percent of the firms surveyed still use DOS.

The good news is that the picture is changing. Accountants have realized the value of the Internet and are now looking to it as a primary resource for business research, downloading software, and identifying, researching, and purchasing business products. A survey conducted by Commerce Clearing House (CCH) in mid-2000 revealed that 96 percent of all accountants have access to the Internet, compared with 51 percent in a survey taken in 1996. The growth is more dramatic when you look at accountants who are using the Web for continuing professional education. Less than 1 percent of accountants surveyed in 1996 used online continuing professional education, compared to 29 percent of accountants in 2000.

There is an abundance of accounting and tax resources on the Internet. These range from accounting news sites, to the Internal Revenue Service site, to sites offering continuing education. Many of the traditional tax services, like CCH and Research Institute of America (RIA), now offer versions on their products on the Internet.

The accounting portal concept is popular with busy professionals who want to find a variety of resources in a single location. Most accounting portals offer industry news, discussion forums, continuing education resources, accounting-related links, and tools such as financial calculators. Most of the portals are free but may require registration to access special features, such as discussion forums. Be aware that several of the accounting portals use the same news feed from Yellow Brix, so in many cases the news sections are not a distinguishing feature.

The major accounting organizations are also organized on the portal concept. For example, CPA Web, a collaborative effort of the American Institute of Certified Public Accountants (AICPA) and state certified public accountant societies, offers a large collection of resources for accountants.

Many of the sites profiled here are so full of content that a short review cannot begin to cover all the material they contained. Some of the Big 5 accounting firm sites listed in this chapter have hundreds of pages that cover the various industry and practice areas, each with its own publications and research papers. Explore these sites using their internal search aids, such as search engines and site maps, to locate information of interest to you.

All sites are presented in alphabetical order. The sites listed in the "First and Foremost" section of this chapter are those that the authors have found to be reliable, well organized, and rich sources of information. Sites offering all or part of the data for free are considered more desirable than sites offering similar data for a fee. "Best of the Rest" sites may focus on a niche area, be fee only, or have limited navigation and output features.

FIRST AND FOREMOST

Accounting Pro2Net

http://accounting.pro2net.com   (Exhibit 9.1)

Free site

Accounting Pro2Net was established in 1995 as AccountingNet. In 2000 AccountingNet morphed into Pro2Net Corporation, reflecting an expansion into other professions, including financial services, human resources, insurance, and law. The accounting part of the site contains a large collection of information of interest to the accounting community. Here you will find an extensive bank of news stories, original articles, and links to a wide range of resources for research, networking, and career development.

Pro2Net's team of experts—editors, publishers, educators, and writers—is what separates this site from many other accounting sites. The original material they provide in the form of news and analysis, commentary, research materials, articles, and educational material is the primary reason to visit this site.

All of the information on the site is free with the exception of the continuing education classes and items for sale in the marketplace area.

What can you expect to find?

- Original articles on a variety of accounting topics
- The NewsLine of current stories selected by the Pro2Net editors

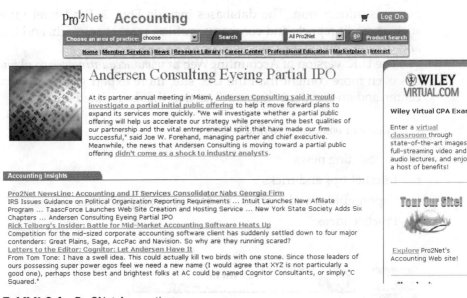

Exhibit 9.1 Pro2Net Accounting

- Continuing education courses
- Audio interviews with industry leaders

AccountingWeb

www.accountingweb.com   (Exhibit 9.2)

Free and Fee-based site

AccountingWeb also follows the accounting portal model. As an online community, AccountingWeb offers the standard discussion forums, news, and articles, all commodity services that it performs very well. The distinguishing features of AccountingWeb are its workshops, expert guides, and its partnership with Brainwave.

The hour-long free workshops are chat sessions with industry experts. Topics have included "Writing a Winning Proposal" and "Clairvoyance—How you can convince your client you can read minds!"

The Expert Guides are articles covering practical topics, such as "PowerPoint Presentations Made Easy" and "Computer Usage Policies." Here you can find a series of online tutorials on using Excel pivot tables written for the U.K. version of AccountingWeb.

Through a partnership with Brainwave, visitors to the AccountingWeb site have access to a pay-as-you-go resource for U.S., Canadian, and international business information. The databases include Dun & Bradstreet information such as credit reports and company profiles, market research, and trademark and demographic data.

The U.K. version of AccountingWeb at *www.accountingweb.co.uk/index.html* has even more content than the U.S. site: more expert guides, a detailed tax center, and an excellent "humour" section that is updated weekly.

What can you expect to find?

- Accounting news
- Internet tips and tricks
- Expert guides and workshops dealing with practical issues
- Practice ideas

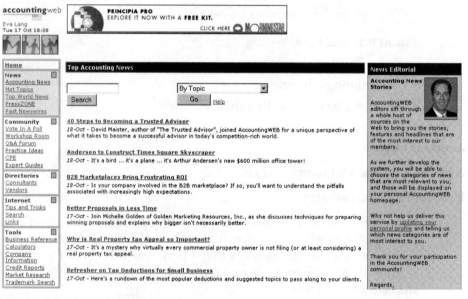

Exhibit 9.2   AccountingWeb

Big Five Sites

Arthur Andersen (*www.arthurandersen.com*)

Deloitte & Touche (*www.dttus.com*)

Ernst & Young (*www.ey.com*)   (Exhibit 9.3)

KPMG (*www.kpmg.com*)   (Exhibit 9.4)

PricewaterhouseCoopers (*www.pwcglobal.com*)   (Exhibit 9.5)

Free and Fee-based sites

The five largest accounting firms have all embraced the Internet. All have multiple websites with varying amounts of information. Count on finding interesting newsletters, many on niche industries and topics, and articles written by Big 5 staffers. Many of the publications available for download are Adobe PDF files preserving the graphics and design of the original print publications. Most of the data is free, but some of the firms sell studies and books published by employees.

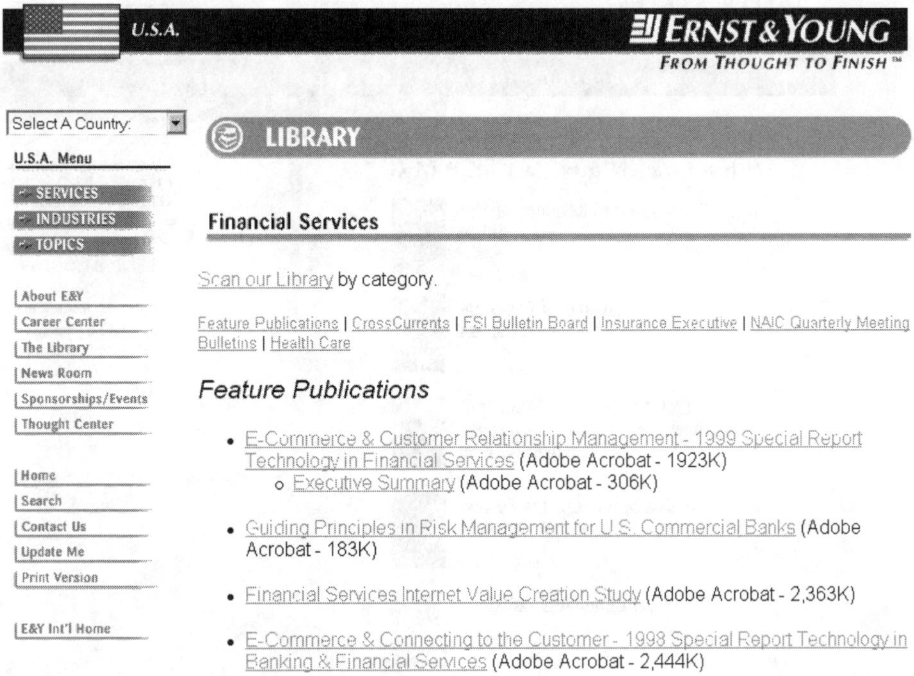

Exhibit 9.3   Big Five (Ernst & Young)

The Arthur Andersen site offers publications and newsletters for download by industry sector, such as the 37-page research report "eB2B in the Financial Services Industry," and by geographic location, such as the 24-page booklet "Call Centres in Belgium: Tax & Legal Aspects." Or click on the resources tab for "Case studies, cool tools, and entrepreneurial stuff."

Deloitte & Touche also makes publications from the firm's different practice areas available on the Web, such as the 22-page "Insurance Industry eCommerce Imperative," and *Healthcare Review,* a monthly newsletter providing interviews and commentaries from leading healthcare executives and policymakers on current health industry issues.

To find publications and newsletters on the Ernst & Young (E&Y) site, click on the Library or Thought Center links. This will take you to publications like *CrossCurrents,* the slick monthly magazine for the financial services industry, and E&Y Insights, a video series of commentaries by Ernst & Young professionals on today's "new economy."

The primary KPMG site at *www.kpmg.com* is a bit stingy with free information, providing only short articles about industry practice areas and a few

Exhibit 9.4   Big Five (KPMG)

videos where KPMG industry experts talk about current issues. To get to the good stuff you will have to go to the sites for the individual practice areas, such as consulting at *www.kpmgconsulting.com.* Here you will find case studies, articles, white papers, and research reports. The sites for individual countries, such as the U.S. site at *www.us.kpmg.com,* also have publications by industry sectors. (One 28-page research report is entitled "Retail Technology in the Next Century: What's In Store for Consumers.")

The PricewaterhouseCoopers (PwC) site also has a number of publications available for download ranging from the 22-page "Electronic Business Outlook—A survey of E-Business Goals, Practices, and Results," to the "Executive

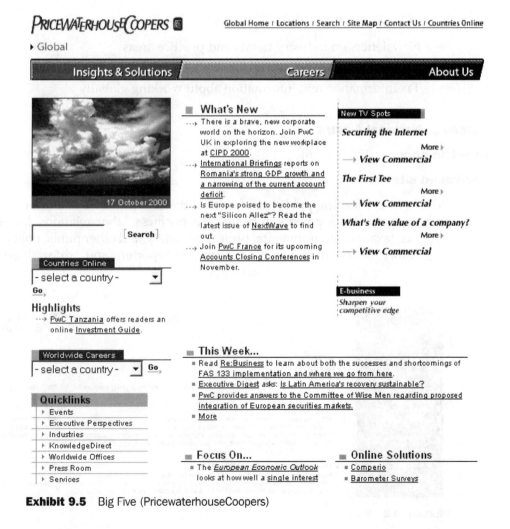

Exhibit 9.5   Big Five (PricewaterhouseCoopers)

Perspective Newsletter." It was surprising to find that PwC did not have e-commerce capability on this site. Those who might be interested in ordering PwC books, such as "Five Frogs on a Log: A CEO's Field Guide to Mergers, Acquisitions & Gut-Wrenching Change," will be directed to Amazon.com.

As mentioned earlier, all the firms have multiple websites. Most have separate websites for the different countries they operate in and for some of the practice areas. Some particularly noteworthy standalone sites from this group include two PwC sites (The Tax News Network at *www.taxnews.com/tnn_public* and the Lodging Research site at *www.lodgingresearch.com*), and two E&Y sites, (the Passport site at *www.doingbusinessin.com* and the TaxCast site at *www. taxcast.com*). The two E&Y sites are discussed later in this chapter in more detail.

What can you expect to find?

- Newsletters on industry trends and practice areas
- Articles, case studies, and working papers
- Tax information and information about working globally

Bureau of National Affairs

www.bna.com   (Exhibit 9.6)

Fee-based site

The BNA is a leading publisher of print and electronic news and information, reporting on developments in healthcare, business, labor relations, law, economics, taxation, environmental protection, safety, and other public policy and regulatory issues. BNA has more than 500 reporters and editors based in

Exhibit 9.6   BNA

Washington, DC, plus correspondents nationwide and in over 40 countries to provide comprehensive, well-written, detailed coverage on these topics.

BNA produces more than 200 news and information services. Among its Web-based products of interest to tax and accounting professionals are:

- TaxCore. Full-text tax regulation and IRS documents updated daily.
- Tax Management Portfolios on the Web. Working papers and bibliographies. Portfolios cover limited liability companies, international pension planning, estate planning, and more.
- Tax Management State Tax Library on the Web. A library of information on state tax issues.
- Tax Management Tax Practice Library. A tax research database including all major primary tax resources, tax analysis, practice tools, and news.

BNA maintains a separate website for the Tax Management products at *www.bnatax.com*.

What can you expect to find?

- Tax research service
- Quality portfolios and analysis of major tax issues
- Practice tools

Commerce Clearing House

www.cch.com

Free and Fee-based site

Commerce Clearing House (CCH) is a major provider of tax and business law information and software. CCH produces approximately 700 publications in print and electronic form for the accounting profession as well as for legal, human resources, banking, securities, insurance, government, and healthcare professionals. The main CCH site at *www.cch.com* is an umbrella for the company's six websites:

1. Federal and State Tax Group (*http://tax.cch.com*)
2. The Business and Finance Site (*http://business.cch.com*)
3. Health Medical and Entitlements (*http://health.cch.com*)
4. Human Resources (*http://hr.cch.com*)
5. Business Owner's Toolkit (*www.toolkit.cch.com*)
6. ProSystemfx (*www.prosystemfx.com*)

Visit the main CCH site to order CCH products online. Otherwise you will want to go directly to one of the CCH subsites. Accounting professionals will be most interested in the Federal and State Tax site (FAST).

The FAST site has some free information, but the primary focus is access to CCH's four online fee-based tax research products: Tax Research Network, taxTracker News, CCH Essentials, and US Master Tax Guide Plus. Here you also can obtain online access to the CCH Financial Planning data service. Several of these databases allow users a free trial period to evaluate the site. The extent of the tax data available is mind-boggling. Suffice it to say that virtually every aspect of taxation, tax law, and tax regulation is covered by a CCH database.

The free information on the FAST site includes discussion forums, a handy online IRS phone book, Applicable Federal Rates by month, weekly feature articles, commentary by CCH editors, and current tax legislation highlights.

The Business Owner's Toolkit site provides a wealth of free data for those running a small business. The extensive online SOHO (Small Office Home Office) guidebook has thousands of pages of information on starting, financing, managing, and marketing a small business. The Business Tools section has free downloadable sample business documents, financial spreadsheet templates, and checklists. There is a small business advice column—Ask Alice— where you can submit questions about running a business.

The other CCH sites offer primarily product information and database access corresponding to each site's focus area along with a selection of free news and articles.

What can you expect to find?

• The motherload of tax information, available for a fee

CPA Journal

www.cpajournal.com　　　(Exhibit 9.7)

Free site

The New York Society of CPAs publishes the monthly *CPA Journal,* a technical-reviewed publication aimed at public practitioners, management, educators, and other accounting professionals. The *CPA Journal* is a long-established (published for 65 years), well-respected publication. An editorial review board composed of CPAs, attorneys, and other professionals helps to keep the quality of the articles high. On the website you will find subscription information and the current issue's table of contents. While there is no access to articles in the current issue, the site has a great archive where you can access most of the *CPA Journal's* excellent articles published since 1989. There is a one-month delay in posting the current month's articles to the archive.

The CPA Journal

Current Issue • About the CPAJ • Search the Archives • NYSSCPA.org

The CPA Journal **High-Net-Worth Issue**

SEPTEMBER **Features**

Charitable Planning for Tax-Favored Retirement Accumulations

By Andrew J. Fair and Melvin L. Maisel

Many high-net-worth individuals intend to use some of their retirement accumulations toward charitable purposes, but there can be unintended consequences if the planning is not done right. The authors present a number of alternative techniques that will safeguard the owner's intent.

Hidden Benefits of the 'Nanny Tax'

By Jo Ann Pinto and Joseph L. LiPari

Many taxpayers disregard (or are ignorant of)the reporting responsibilities imposed by the "nanny tax." In some cases, the financial burden of compliance is not a great as one might think.

Exhibit 9.7 The CPA Journal
Courtesy of *The CPA Journal*, www.cpajournal.com.

What can you expect to find?

- Great articles from one of the accounting profession's most respected publications on topics ranging from auditing to consulting

Electronic Accountant

www.electronicaccountant.com (Exhibit 9.8)

Free site

The Electronic Accountant site is a product of Faulkner and Gray, the publisher who brought you the biweekly news tabloid *Accounting Today* and the monthly slick magazines *Practical Accountant* and *Accounting Technology.*

The site features accounting news stories from Newswire, a daily news feature written by accounting editors, and a selection of feature articles on the accounting industry from the magazines previously mentioned and other magazines published by Faulkner and Gray. There is a great news archive of Faulkner and Gray news stories dating back to 1996. Also on the site are links, product information, continuing education resources, and discussion forums.

The Wall Street Window stock market section covers stocks of interest to the accounting community, such as Robert Half and H&R Block. The Career center provides job listings, CPA Exam information, and salary data. The special reports section features a number of in-depth articles, such as "Online CPE

Exhibit 9.8 The Electronic Accountant

Changes the Face of Tax, Accounting Education," but, unfortunately, none of the special reports is dated. Content on the site is generally excellent but the site design is cluttered, making it hard to find what you want. Also, the search capability of the site is inadequate.

Come to the Electronic Accountant for the excellent Newswire and to read stories from the current issues of Faulkner and Gray publications. These features set this site apart from the other accounting sites.

What can you expect to find?

- Cover stories from the current issues of *Practical Accountant*, *Accounting Today*, and *Accounting Technology*
- Well-written news stories on the hot topics in accounting
- Discussion forums on accounting and auditing topics

Internal Revenue Service

www.irs.gov

www.irs.gov/prod/bus_info/tax_pro/index.html   (Exhibit 9.9)

Free sites

You have to give the IRS credit for making an interesting, informative, and amusing website. The wealth of information, the campy design (e.g., click on the image of a bandage to get to the help section), and the ease of navigation could almost give you a warm and fuzzy feeling about the nation's tax collectors. The IRS has done a much better job than many other federal government agencies when it comes to organizing large amounts of information. You can skip the basic consumer tax information on the home page and go directly to a section prepared for tax professionals, or use the IRS Site Tree at *www.irs.ustreas.gov/prod/search/site_tree.html* to help you negotiate the thousands of pages of data on this site.

From the Tax Professionals Corner you can access advance releases of IRS Revenue Rulings, Revenue Procedures, and other technical items before they are published in the *Internal Revenue Bulletin.* The "Tax Law Issues, Nibbles & Bytes" section contains links to all of the most technical references on the site. There is a whole section on the IRS e-filing program for tax professionals at *www.irs.ustreas.gov/prod/elec_svs/ets2.html.* The Tax Professionals Corner is also the primary source for IRS tax filing forms, including drafts of new forms before they are released. You also can subscribe to two current awareness products, the Digital Dispatch and the Local News Net.

Other sections of the IRS site cover topics such as Regulations in Plain English, Tax Statistics, Tax Information for Businesses, Forms and Publications, and News.

What can you expect to find?

- Information on every aspect of tax filing
- Tax forms
- IRS regulations
- Aggregate statistics compiled for tax returns
- IRS publications

The Internal Revenue Service's **THE DIGITAL DAILY** *Presents ...*

TAX PROFESSIONAL'S *Corner*

The *Tax Professional's Corner* provides links to items on the *Digital Daily* which are helpful to the tax professional. We want to make it easy for tax professionals to find everything they need.

[Click for Text Only Version]

News For the Tax Professional

Check here for the latest news of interest to Tax Professionals. We will update the page periodically as the news comes in.

Tax Law Issues, Nibbles & Bytes

Here's the beef! We've linked to all of the most technical references on our site and will add new items as soon as available. Check out our new Advance Notices for Tax Professionals.

Administrative Information & Resources

Forms and Pubs

Official IRS Forms, Instructions, & Publications

If you need to get a particular tax product, this is the right place.

Early Release DRAFTS of Forms

You can now get drafts of most major tax forms months before they are officially released. You can also provide comments on the draft forms before they are finalized.

Exhibit 9.9   The Internal Revenue Service's "The Digital Daily"

Tax Analysts

www.tax.org/defaultf.htm   (Exhibit 9.10)

Free and Fee-based site

Tax Analysts products are a great value for tax research on or off the Internet. The only nonprofit tax research vendor, Tax Analysts offers tax research products through its website and through the Tax Library (*www.taxlibrary.com*) site, which Tax Analysts purchased in 2000.

TaxBase is the premier tax research product from Tax Analysts. Subscribers to TaxBase on the Web get access to current awareness products such as Tax Notes Today as well as the TaxBase Federal Research Library, which, according to Tax Analysts, has more tax information than the IRS. Also included are state tax products and a library of 40,000 court opinions on tax issues. If the $3,500 price tag for annual access to TaxBase is a bit steep for your budget, consider the Tax Library. Tax Library does not have the depth of TaxBase, but it does offer a large amount of federal source material as well as a weekly TaxPractice online magazine and the Practice Alert online newsletter for $300 per year. Other products accessible on the Tax Analysts site include state and international tax databases and specialty publications. Tax Analysts supplies tax information to a number of other vendors, including Lexis, Dialog, and Westlaw.

Exhibit 9.10 Tax.org

The Tax Analysts site also has a significant amount of free content. The daily Tax Wire (*www.tax.org/TaxWire/taxwiref.htm*) covers current tax stories. Readings in Federal Tax Policy is a compilation of some of the best articles published in *Tax Notes* magazine. Feature stories cover international, state, and e-commerce issues. There is also a directory of tax professionals, reports on lobbying and legislative activities, and the ever-popular collection of presidential tax returns.

What can you expect to find?

- Voluminous amounts of tax information—regulations, forms, news stories, rates, court cases
- Current stories from *Tax Notes,* the federal tax journal of record
- Quotes from the famous and not-so-famous about the vagaries of taxation

BEST OF THE REST

Accountant's World

www.accountantsworld.com

Free site

This site has some of the features of an accounting portal, such as discussion forums, calculators, and news stories, but it lacks original content. The core of the site is a nearly exhaustive list of links to tax, accounting, and other business sites. To add value to this link list, Accountant's World solicits and publishes reviews from readers. However, at the date of this writing few sites had reviews. If you are looking for an accounting site, chances are there is a link to it here.

AICPA Online

www.aicpa.org

Free site

AICPA Online is the current home of the AICPA on the Internet. But things are changing. In 2000 the AICPA announced plans for a major Internet initiative, a new collaborative small business portal site in partnership with state CPA societies. As an interim step in July 2000, the AICPA launched Cpaweb.org in conjunction with the 50 state CPA societies. This site is a transitional website and is a first step in the move toward the Internet portal, "cpa2biz," to be launched in 2001. The primary content on the CPAweb.org site is InfoBytes, the AICPA's educational service that provides "all-you-can-eat" courses for $95 a year for AICPA members.

The current AICPA Online site provides detailed information on the institute's operations and programs, including legislative and regulatory developments affecting the accounting profession. There are also career resources, including a job bank and information on hiring trends in the industry. The AICPA-published *Journal of Accountancy* is available online. Selected articles are available for free from each issue beginning in 1997. An online index covers stories since 1996.

Audit Net

www.auditnet.org

Free site

Audit information is not plentiful on the Internet, but Audit Net pulls together a collection of resources that auditors will find helpful. Audit Net has dozens of audit programs available for download from the site. Auditors will also find job postings and other career resources along with information on audit training programs.

CPA Net

www.cpanet.com

Free site

CPANet is primarily a resource directory of websites that are of interest to the accounting profession. A discussion forum and a news feed make this site sort of a "portal lite." Site content is free, but users must be registered to receive a newsletter and access the forums.

Environmental Accounting Project

www.epa.gov/opptintr/acctg

Free site

This site was launch by the United States Environmental Protection Agency (EPA) in 1992 to help businesses account for environmental costs. On the site you can find a number of publications designed to educate users on the economic benefits of environmental concern. Resources include full-text papers, surveys, reports, and case studies on managerial accounting practices, corporate decision-making processes, environmental policy reforms, and profitability indicators.

EY Passport

www.doingbusinessin.com

Free site

This site, developed by Ernst & Young, offers a wealth of tax and business knowledge on more than 140 countries, updated quarterly. Users can access a series of country profiles tailored to help executives do business in specific countries. They also can access a worldwide corporate tax guide and information on the tax implications of relocation to other countries. The site also contains *Tax News International,* a quarterly digest of tax information for more than 50 countries.

EY TaxCast

www.taxcast.com

Free site

EY TaxCast was developed by Ernst & Young as a source of information for tax-related issues. Be sure to check the E&Y Tax News section, where you will find hundreds of E&Y Tax Alerts on various topics, and the Knowledge Center for links to E&Y tax guides and analyses. Access to the TaxCast Executive Edition for corporate tax professionals has been folded into the E&Y Online site at *www.ey.com/ernieonlinetaxadvisor.*

Federal Tax Law

www.taxsites.com/federal.html

Free site

Federal tax law resources are a key part of tax research. Many of the resources are available from the government agencies that publish them. So you will find the U.S. tax code at the House of Representatives website and the Code of Federal Regulations on the Government Printing Office site. The Tax Sites page on Federal Tax Law provides links to these and other federal tax resources from a single page. There are also links to commercial sites that offer or comment on federal tax regulations.

Tax Sites has more than just links to federal tax information. Dennis Schmidt, a professor of accounting at the University of Northern Iowa, designed this comprehensive index as a "starting point" for most tax and accounting subject searches. Schmidt does the two basic things necessary to make a link site work—he lists quality sites and updates them frequently.

While this seems obvious, it is rare to find a well-maintained link site. Check the Tax Sites home page at *www.taxsites.com* for links to more tax resources.

FTA State Tax Rates

www.taxadmin.org/fta/rate/tax_stru.html

Free site

The membership of the Federation of Tax Administrators (FTA) includes the principal tax collection agencies of all 50 states. On this website you can find current information on income tax rates by states. There is also information on sales and excise taxes and surveys of tax practices by state. One section of the site (*www.taxadmin.org/fta/FORMS.ssi*) provides tax forms for every state.

RIA Tax

www.riatax.com

Fee-based site

In its current incarnation, RIA is a subsidiary of Thomson Tax and Accounting formed by the merger of the Research Institute of America, Computer Language Research, and Warren, Gorham & Lamont. This combined organization is now the world's largest provider of tax research.

There is some free information at the RIA site. You can find some current news stories and access to selected articles from journals published by Warren, Gorham & Lamont. But for tax research, you will need to subscribe to Checkpoint, RIA's Web-based tax research system. Checkpoint covers a vast amount of data, including federal editorial materials, state and local tax information, estate planning materials, IRS rulings and releases, federal court decisions, and pending and enacted tax legislation.

RIA's sister company Warren Gorham & Lamont offers a number of nontax financial and accounting products as a part of its Corporate Finance Network at *www.wglcorpfinance.com.* Here you can access fee-based services, including "SEC Compliance," "GAAP Compliance," "Internal Auditing," "Finance Professional," and "FASB Database."

World Tax

www.taxresources.com/html/taxsites/foreign.html

Free site

The World Tax page is a great starting place for learning about the tax systems in 190 different countries. It provides links to the major free tax resources in each country. There is a database of free tax resources, searchable by country using pull-down menus, along with links to articles and discussions of global tax issues. A similar site with good international information is the Taxes Around the World site at *www.paradine.com/worldtax/index.html*.

CHAPTER **10**

International Business

Jan Davis Tudor

Creating a comprehensive collection of websites for international business research is a monumental task. Each country is unique, as are its information sources. In addition, many countries do not share the United States' democratic attitude toward sharing information, and many governments have not compiled and archived data, let alone made it available to the public. Needless to say, researching a foreign company, country, or industry may be difficult, and the research process will probably take a lot longer than usual. However, your efforts may be rewarded, as more and more information-rich sites from countries around the world are made available. One more caveat that should not be surprising: Many of the sites you find will not be in English. If you do not speak the language in question, have a trusty dictionary or a friend by your side.

In order to facilitate research involving a foreign country or industry, many librarians, information specialists, and businesspeople have created metasites, or portals, that serve as great starting places for your research. These individuals have scoured the Web, selected and reviewed the best websites, and organized them for your successful research pleasure.

Because so many good sites exist for global business research, the authors recommend Sheri Lanza's upcoming book, *International Business Information on the Web*, published by Information Today and available in the spring of 2001.

All sites are presented in alphabetical order. The sites listed in the "First and Foremost" section of this chapter are those that the authors have found to be reliable, well organized, and rich sources of information. Sites offering all or part of the data for free are considered more desirable than sites offering similar data for a fee. "Best of the Rest" sites may focus on a niche area, be fee only, or have limited navigation and output features.

FIRST AND FOREMOST

American Chambers of Commerce Abroad

www.uschamber.org/International/Chambers+Abroad/
Chambers+Abroad+Directory.htm

Free site

American Chambers of Commerce Abroad (AmChams) are voluntary associations of U.S. individuals doing business in a particular country and firms and individuals of countries that operate in the United States. Eighty-six AmChams in 76 countries are affiliated with the U.S. Chamber of Commerce and were established to advance U.S. business interests abroad.

What can you expect to find?

- A directory of AmChams and their websites; each site provides business-related publications and services for the country in which it is located

Bureau van Dijk

www.bvdep.com   (Exhibit 10.1)

Free and Fee-based site

Bureau van Dijk is an established Belgium-based company whose databases provide extensive information on European companies. This is an excellent tool for targeting companies within a particular industry or accessing detailed financial data. Researchers can target companies of interest by using the free directory. This directory provides access to all 6.5 million companies contained in Bureau van Dijk databases. A summary has information for every company provided, with links to the full reports.

What can you expect to find?

- Detailed company reports on 6 million European companies
- 24,500 listed companies worldwide
- 11,100 banks worldwide

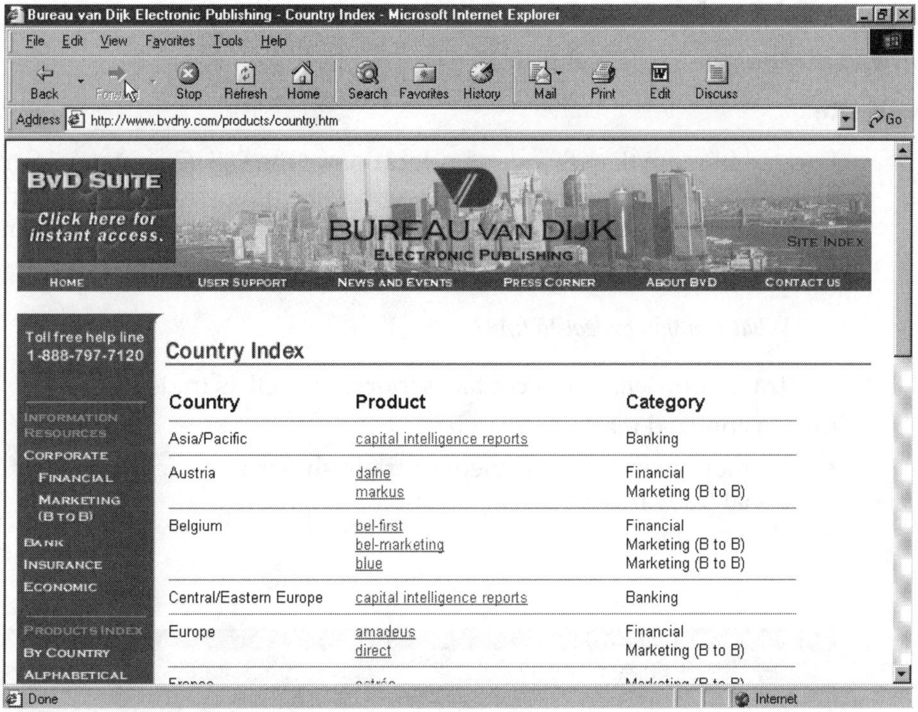

Exhibit 10.1 Bureau van Dijk

- 4,300 insurance companies worldwide
- Statistical databases
- Directories, technical, legal, and bibliographical databases

Business Information Sources on the Internet: Country Information

www.dis.strath.ac.uk/business/index.html

Free site

This site, compiled and maintained by the Department of Information Science of the University of Strathclyde in Glasgow, Scotland, is a fantastic starting point for international business research projects.

What can you expect to find?

- Links to worldwide company profiles and financial information
- Links to international statistical, economic, export data, and news sources
- Links to commercial market research companies throughout the world

Commercial Service—U.S. Department of Commerce

www.usatrade.gov   (Exhibit 10.2)

Free site

Located in more than 80 overseas locations, "the U.S. Commercial Service is a global network of 1,700 trade professionals helping you to reach your international business goals." The Commercial Service's mission is to increase the number of U.S. firms that benefit from international trade.

What can you expect to find?

- Trade counseling and contact services as well as trade leads
- Customized market research
- Promotion and management of trade shows and organization of international trade missions

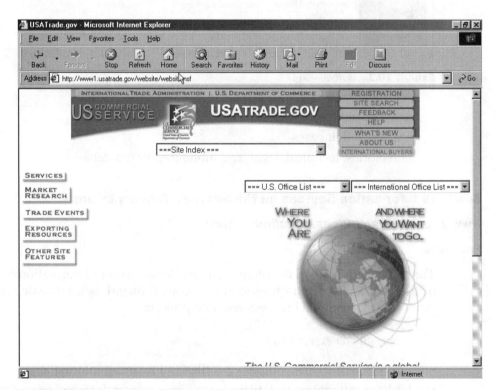

Exhibit 10.2   Commercial Service—U.S. Department of Commerce

CorporateInformation

www.corporateinformation.com (Exhibit 10.3)

Free site

This well-organized site serves as a wonderful starting point for international research on companies and industries. From the home page researchers can search by industry, country, or company name. For example, by entering "Automotive" in the industry box and "Argentina" in the country box, researchers will retrieve a list of sources relating to the automotive industry in Argentina. The search results contain not only a three-page industry summary but also links to a market research report, an industry update from Mercosul, and a list of automotive firms in the country and links to their websites.

What can you expect to find?

- Links to hundreds of sites relating to industries and companies around the world
- Country-specific background information, exchange rates, stock exchange quotes, and economic indicators

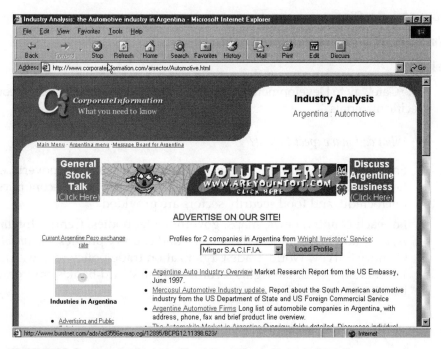

Exhibit 10.3 Industry Analysis: The Automotive Industry in Argentina
Copyright 2000 The Winthrop Corporation. All rights reserved.

Country Net

www.countrynet.com

Fee-based site

"The online information center for expatriates and business travelers." This site is sponsored by Arthur Andersen, the Economist Intelligence Unit (EIU), and Craighead.com. The site was designed to provide "a comprehensive new online information service designed to give expatriates, international road warriors and global nomads all the information they need to relocate and operate knowledgeably, safely and effectively in new countries, cultures and business markets worldwide."

What can you expect to find?

- Country profiles containing a country overview and descriptions of local business culture and customs, expatriate tax guide, customs and import duty regulations, and medical and security reports
- A database of links to more than 200 other useful websites for each country

Eldis Country Profiles

http://nt1.ids.ac.uk/eldis/newcountry.htm

Free site

"The Gateway to Development Information" provides "quick access to country-specific materials."

What can you expect to find?

- For each country, profiles on the agriculture, environment, poverty, education, gender, health and population, governance, trade, economics, aid, microcredit, and food security sectors are provided.
- For each country, news, maps, governmental bodies, Central Intelligence Agency and International Monetary Fund country profiles, *Financial Times* Country Survey, World Trade Organization trade policy review, Amnesty International's human rights record, and the World Bank's environmental profile are provided.

European Union "Business Resources"

www.eurunion.org/infores/business/business.htm

Free site

"The European Commission Delegation does not provide assistance for business development, commercial contacts or investment possibilities in Europe"; however, it has provided links to many sources of European business information relating to doing business in Europe.

What can you expect to find?

- Business directories
- European trade associations
- Investment opportunities in Europe
- Links to the chambers of commerce of European Union members in the United States
- U.S. government services for exporters, and U.S. private sector organizations
- The "One Stop Internet Shop for Business"—an additional site that contains overviews of relevant legislation and business advice

EXPORT@11.net

www.exportall.net

Free site

Exportall is a compendium of export and international business information on the Net. Its aim is to provide comprehensive links to business information sources for over 200 countries.

What can you expect to find?

- The site consists of a general directory and a country directory. The general directory is organized in broad topics, such as "business & industry" and "news & media."
- The country directory features a home page for every country in the world and helps you find information in a number of subcategories, such as "business & industry," "facts & figures," "government & politics," "news & media," and so on.

Global Business Web

www.GlobalBusinessWeb.com

Free site

"Global Business Web is a free international business portal to make contacts, do research, promote your company and conduct business." Developed by Link Interactive, this site serves as a portal of resources relating to doing business internationally. It contains over 5,000 links to articles, discussions, services, and resources from all over the world. The site is considered by the University of Kansas to be one of the "Top 10 International Resources on the Web" because it is provides thousands of maps, magazines, and global business resources.

What can you expect to find?

- Links to company directories
- Current news from Associated Press and a political risk newsletter
- A discussion forum where users can post questions about doing business around the world
- Links to sites of trade leads
- A database of over 50,000 events, trade shows, and trade missions from around the world as well as a trade show newsletter
- Links to imports and exports databases

Global Financial Data and Resources Locators

www.ntu.edu.sg/library/biz/financial.htm

Free site

This site is a "Singapore-based site that provides a huge selection of links to material on international finance, banking, stock exchanges. International in focus yet an excellent gateway to Asian financial contents." Global Financial Data and Resources Locators serves as a compendium of links for international business research and is organized by subject.

What can you expect to find?

- Links to stock exchange and security market sites worldwide
- Links to sites containing data on interest rates, currency, and exchange rates

GLOBUS and the National Trade Data Bank

www.stat-usa.gov/tradtest.nsf   (Exhibit 10.4)

Free and Fee-based site

This site is a must-stop for those interested in doing business overseas or finding out about a particular market or industry. Most of the information is gathered and published by agencies of the U.S. government.

What can you expect to find?

- Extensive country and market research at a very low cost
- Up-to-date and historical "global business opportunity leads"
- International trade statistics, such as U.S. exports and imports by commodity and country
- Current exchange rates

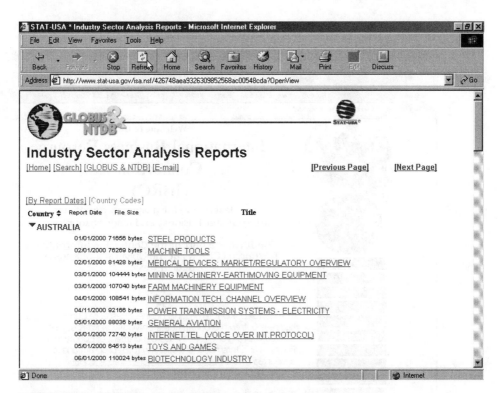

Exhibit 10.4   STAT-USA—Industry Sector Analysis Reports
STAT-USA®, STAT-USA/Internet™, NTDB®, National Trade Data Bank®, and GLOBUS®. All are International Class Trademarks held by STAT-USA, U.S. Department of Commerce.

- Current press releases regarding U.S. import and export price indexes, U.S. Department of Agriculture export sales, and U.S. International Trade in goods and services

International Business Resource Connection

www.ibrc.bschool.ukans.edu   (Exhibit 10.5)

Free site

"The International Business Resource Connection (IBRC) helps small and medium-size companies broaden their international business skills and explore available international trade opportunities." Run by the University of Kansas, the IBRC is an excellent and comprehensive collection of international trade and business resources on the Internet. In fact, search engine Lycos rated it the number-one International Business website in May 1999.

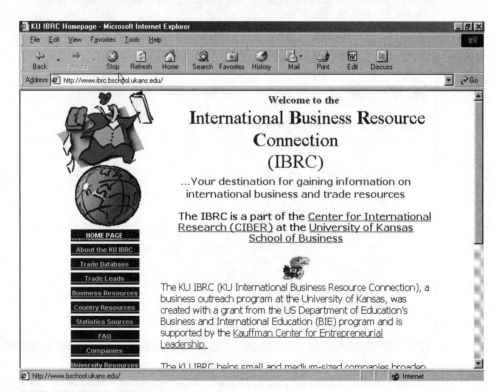

Exhibit 10.5   KU IBRC Homepage

What can you expect to find?

- Trade databases
- Detailed information on every country's business, government, and travel resources
- International trades statistics

International Business Resources on the WWW

http://ciber.bus.msu.edu/busres.htm   (Exhibit 10.6)

Free site

International Business Resources on the WWW is a directory compiled and maintained by the Michigan State University, Center for International Business Education and Research (CIBER). The site contains hundreds of links to global business information sites and is particularly useful because it contains only those sites that provide value-added information. The entire site is searchable by keyword and is also organized by subject.

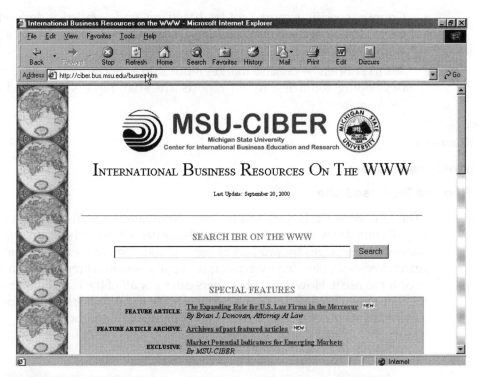

Exhibit 10.6 MSU-CIBER International Business Resources on the WWW

What can you expect to find?

- Links to U.S. and international news, periodicals, journals, articles, and research papers
- Links to regional and country-specific statistical and information sources
- International trade information and trade leads
- Company directories and Yellow Pages

International Trade Center

www.intracen.org

Free and Fee-based site

The International Trade Center is an executing agency of the United Nations Development Programme and, through its website, provides a set of tools for monitoring national and sectoral trade performance.

What can you expect to find?

- Country-specific export profiles based on trade statistics derived from COMTRADE of the United Nations Statistics Division, the world's largest trade database
- "Market Briefs"—concise market reports on export products of interest to developing countries; recent reports are $100, reports published before 1995 are free

Kompass

www.kompass.com

Free and fee-based site

"The Link Between Buyers and Sellers," Kompass is a well-established directory of companies and products from 70 countries. Researchers can search in a variety of languages by product or service and company or trade name. The search also can be limited by geographic area. Users must register with the site in order to use it. However, subscribers can view all of the listings contained in the database. This directory is an excellent way to find basic information about a company or pull together a list of a company's competitors.

What can you expect to find?

- Information on 1.5 million companies, and 23 million key products, 600,000 trade and brand names, and 2.9 million executive names

Latin American Network Information Center

http://lanic.utexas.edu

Free site

The Latin American Network Information Center (LANIC) is a well-established metasite of information to, from, or on Latin America. LANIC is affiliated with the Institute of Latin American Studies at the University of Texas at Austin, and the institute's editors have reviewed over 12,000 unique Internet sites relating to Latin America.

What can you expect to find?

- The full spectrum of information: county-specific, economic, education, government, libraries and reference, media and communication, Internet and computing, science, social sciences, humanities, and society and culture

Tradeport

www.tradeport.org/ts

Free site

TradePort is a great site for trade information, trade leads, and company databases. Funding for the site was provided by the U.S. Department of Commerce Economic Development Administration, and significant assistance was provided by the U.S. Commercial Service, the California Trade and Commerce Agency, and other sponsors. The "Country Library" allows researchers to find information for just about any country in the world, and the "Industry Library" provides links to trade associations and trade leads.

What can you expect to find?

- Demographic and political background information, market research, and industry sector analysts' reports
- Economic policies, trade practices, trends, and outlooks
- Information on how to market U.S. products and services and a list of leading sectors for U.S. exports and investment
- Trade regulations and standards and information on the investment climate and trade and project financing
- Links to chambers of commerce, foreign service posts, and embassies
- An "Industry Library" that contains links to dozens of sites containing information on the following industries: Agriculture and Processed Foods, Computer and Related Electronics, Environmental Technologies, Multimedia

and Information Technologies, Telecommunications, and Bioscience/Bio-medical Technologies and Instruments

The Wall Street Journal

www.wsj.com

Fee-based site

Subscribers to the online version of *The Wall Street Journal* have access to the entire Dow Jones Publication Library, which contains current and archived articles from thousands of trade journals and newspapers from around the world. Dow Jones' recent merger with Reuters increases the number of international publications available to researchers. Subscriptions for the online version are $59 a year or $29 a year if one subscribes to the print version. Articles from the Dow Jones Publications Library run $2.95 each.

BEST OF THE REST

1001 Sites.com

www.1001sites.com

Free site

"The Arab Internet Directory," a metasite of links to thousands of sites in the Arab World. It is searchable by keyword and business category.

Arab World Online

www.awo.net

Free site

Arab World Online contains current news, articles, and detailed business-related information for 22 countries.

Asia Big

www.asiabig.com

Free site

Business and industrial guides, as well as free articles on the business climate in Hong Kong, Jakarta, Klang Valley, Malasia, Philippines, Singapore, and Taiwan are provided. The site is also searchable by company, product, service, and geographic area.

Background Notes

www.state.gov/index.cfm

Free site

Published by the U.S. State Department, Background Notes provides information about a country's geography, people, government, economy, history, politics, travel, and business. Organized by region, then by country, a Background Note is available for just about every country in the world.

Bank Hapoalim

www.bankhapoalim.co.il

Free site

Israeli Bank Hapoalim's website provides links to profiles of leading Tel Aviv Stock Exchange companies and Israeli companies trading on the London and U.S. exchanges. Also included are weekly and daily reviews of the Israeli capital markets, analysts' reports for selected companies, daily stocks and bonds prices, and updated economic forecasts. The site is presented in four languages: Hebrew, Russian, Spanish, and English.

BolagsFakta

www.bolagsfakta.se/default.html

Free site

BolagsFakta is a database of Swedish company annual reports and other financial information. Information is presented in Swedish.

Braby's Red Index

www.brabys.co.za

Free site

A business-to-business directory for southern Africa. Seventy percent of the companies covered in Braby's Red Index are small to medium size.

Canadian Business Map

http://commercecan.ic.gc.ca

Free site

> This Canadian metasite provides links to the provinces and municipalities of Canada.

China Big

www.chinabig.com

Free site

> This metasite offers links to a variety of Chinese business information.

China Online

www.chinaonline.com

Free site

> China Online provides access to a number of economic and business sources. Brief industry outlooks and current news is free, but customized reports incur a fee.

Company Records Online

www.carol.co.uk

Free and Fee-based site

> Company Records Online (CAROL) is a "free corporate on-line service offering one point access to company annual reports" for companies in the United Kingdom. The database is searchable by company name and industry grouping.

The Embassy Web

www.embpage.org/index.html

Free site

> A searchable database that contains 50,000 addresses, phone numbers and email addresses of diplomatic posts worldwide.

Europages: The European Business Directory

www.europages.com

Free site

> Europages is a Yellow Pages–type directory of 500,000 companies in 30 European countries. The site is searchable by product, service, and company name. Researchers also can search through a list of business categories, such as "Fruits & Vegetables" or "Building Materials."

EY Passport

www.doingbusinessin.com

Free site

> This site, developed by Ernst & Young, offers a wealth of tax and business knowledge on more than 140 countries, updated quarterly. Users can access a series of country profiles tailored to help executives do business in specific countries. They also can access a worldwide corporate tax guide and information on the tax implications of relocation to other countries. The site also contains *Tax News International,* a quarterly digest of tax information for more than 50 countries.

Global Business Centre

www.glreach.com/gbc

Free site

> "The Global Business Centre is a resource that provides links to interesting Web sites throughout the world, especially those not written in English." The site is organized by subject within each language: business, culture, online publications and e-zines, leisure, jobs, shopping, and travel.

Guide to International Investing

www.disclosure-investor.com

Free site

> This publication by Disclosure describes the disclosure practices for public companies throughout the world.

Hieros Gamos: The Comprehensive Law and Government Portal

www.hg.org/1table.html

Free site

> Hieros Gamos was one of the first legal and government sites on the Internet. Despite its cluttered home page, it is a comprehensive starting point for law-related information. Its comprehensive search engine searches 11,000 law and government sites and provides information on "every country and government on earth."

Hoover's Online

www.hoovers.com   (Exhibit 10.7)

Free and Fee-based site

> While Hoover's is known for its in-depth profiles of U.S. public companies, the site also provides quite a bit of information on selected international companies. In fact, the Hoover's database covers 65,000 companies around the world.

International Statistical Agencies

www.census.gov/main/www/stat_int.html

Free site

> Compiled by the U.S. Census Bureau, this site provides links to the national statistical agencies for dozens of countries.

Latin Supplier

http://eee.cdmex.com

Free site

> Latin Supplier is a directory of 10,492 manufacturers and 1,876 service providers in Latin American countries. Each company listing contains the company name, address, and telephone numbers, contact name if the person speaks English, e-mail address, product/service, and number of employees.

Exhibit 10.7   Granada Compass PLC Capsule—Hoover's UK
Courtesy of Hoover's Online (*www.hoovers.com*).

Mark Bernkopf's Central Banking Resource Center

http://patriot.net/~bernkopf

Free site

Regional and central bank websites often provide important information about a country's economic condition. This website provides a comprehensive collection of links to the central banks of the world, such as the Banco Central of Nicaragua.

Mbendi: Africa's Leading Website

www.mbendi.co.za

Free site

Consulting firm Mbendi Information Services Ltd.'s website provides country, company, and business-related information for every country in Africa. In addition, the site considers itself "one of the world's top mining, energy and international trade websites." A major objective of the site is to help the business community identify African business opportunities.

New Zealand Companies Office Database

www.companies.govt.nz

Fee-based site

This site provides detailed financial data on registered New Zealand companies. Report prices start at $4NZ.

Orientation Global Network

www.orientation.com

Free site

A portal of worldwide information, this site's tag line is "Think Globally, Search Locally." The home page is divided into three sections that include links to regional information, current news and weather, travel information, and a site search option. Perhaps for research purposes users will focus on the first section, which contains six regional categories: Africa, Asia, Central and Eastern Europe, Latin America and the Caribbean; the Middle East; and Oceania. From this six categories four subsections are presented: Today, Travel, Community, and Web Directory. Because the list of links presented under each country can be quite extensive, the authors suggest using the "Search Orientation" featured on each page.

Planet Business

www.planetbiz.com

Free site

Planet Business provides links to the Yellow Pages of just about every country in the world. It is organized by country.

System for Electronic Document Analysis and Retrieval

www.sedar.com/homepage.htm

Free site

> The System for Electronic Document Analysis and Retrieval (SEDAR) is the electronic filing system for public companies and mutual funds in Canada. The SEDAR website contains copies of the disclosure documents filed in the system as well as profiles containing basic information about each company or mutual fund group.

Thomas Register of European Manufacturers

www.tipcoeurope.be

Free and Fee-based site

> The European counterpart to the *Thomas Register of American Manufactures,* this directory contains listings for 180,000 industrial suppliers in 17 European countries. Researchers can search by company name in one of six languages or work down a list of 10,000 industrial product descriptions. The site is free to search but registration is required. Each listing contains company contact information and a link to the company's website and catalog, if available.

WebTop.com

www.webtop.com

Free site

> Formerly EuroFerret, WebTop is a directory of over 30 million documents. A search on "Poland and Vodka" retrieved links to the Polish Vodka website and various distillers in Poland. The site is searchable in several languages.

World Factbook

www.odci.gov/cia/publications/factbook/index.html

Free site

> Published by the Central Intelligence Agency, the *World Factbook* has been a long-standing source of background information on countries. Each chapter includes data on the country's economy, government, communications, geography, people, transportation, and military.

Index